SCHOOL
TO
STARTUP

SCHOOL TO STARTUP

NAVIGATING THE PATH OF ENTREPRENEURSHIP

ROHIT SINHA

Vitasta

Published by
Renu Kaul Verma
Vitasta Publishing Pvt Ltd
4348/4C, Ansari Road, Daryaganj
New Delhi - 110 002
info@vitastapublishing.com

ISBN: 978-81-19670-77-2
© Rohit Sinha
First Edition 2024
MRP ₹ 250

All Rights Reserved.
No part of this publication may be reproduced, stored in a retrieval system, or transmitted in any form, or by any means–electronic, mechanical, photocopying, recording or otherwise–without the prior permission of the publisher.
The views and opinions expressed in this book are the author's own. The publisher is in no way responsible for the same. While every effort has been made to verify the accuracy of the information presented, the publisher disclaims any responsibility for errors or omissions.

Edited by Vichitra Goel
Typeset by Rohit Gautam
Cover Design by Maida Y
Printed by Vikas Computer and Printers, New Delhi

CONTENTS

Preface   *vii*

Introduction   *ix*

The Power of an Entrepreneurial Mindset   1

Identifying Your Passion and Purpose   12

Developing Essential Skills for Success   21

Building a Solid Foundation   31

Launching Your Startup   43

Marketing and Branding Strategies   54

Sales and Growth Strategies   66

Managing Risks and Failures   80

Building a Strong Visitor Culture   91

Scaling and Exiting Strategies   105

Appendix: Resources and Tools   *119*

PREFACE

Dear Reader,

Welcome to an insightful reading of *School to Startup: Navigating the Path of Entrepreneurship*. I am thrilled to have you accompany me on this exciting journey into the entrepreneurship world. My name is Rohit Sinha, and I am a young entrepreneur who has poured his heart and soul into creating this book with some help from Artificial Intelligence.

The idea for the book was born during my school days when the stories of successful entrepreneurs and their journeys enthralled me. Intrigued by the scope and challenges of a business venture, I embarked on a quest to learn from the field experts. Over the years, I have immersed myself in research, diligently studying various aspects of entrepreneurship and compiling significant notes from my learning with the help of Artificial Intelligence.

My vision for this book is simple yet profound–to share the wealth of knowledge and the experiences I have gained with aspiring entrepreneurs like you. I believe that by empowering each other, we can collectively make a long-lasting impact on the world.

The spirit of collaboration, support, and sharing is at the crux of this book. I firmly believe that as we uplift one another, we contribute to the growth of the flourishing entrepreneurial ecosystem.

I strongly believe that knowledge should not be confined; it should be easily accessible and available. With this in mind, I made the visualisation to publish this book, making all I have learned and noted during my entrepreneurial years available to all. My sincere hope is that it serves as a valuable resource for your journey as well.

As we dive into these pages, I invite you to be open-minded, curious, and ready to take action. Whether you are a student with a dream or an aspiring entrepreneur with a vision, I reassure you that this book has been designed to be a practical and inspiring guide.

Together, let us embark on this transformative journey, embracing the challenges and opportunities that come our way. With the knowledge shared here, I am confident we can turn ideas into reality and contribute to a brighter future.

Thank you for joining me on this quest. Let's make a difference together, one step at a time.

INTRODUCTION
A Note on Rohit Sinha

Welcome to *School to Startup: Navigating the Path of Entrepreneurship*. This book is your guide to transitioning from the structured school environment to the dynamic and challenging world of startups. By developing an entrepreneurial mindset and equipping yourself with the necessary skills, you can transform your passion into a successful venture. Get ready to embark on an exciting journey of self-discovery, innovation, and growth.

The Seed of Curiosity

When Rohit was in grade 5-6, he heard the word 'startup' for the first time on a news channel. Intrigued by the term, he approached his parents to find its meaning. His parents explained that a startup is any new marketing venture initiated by an entrepreneur with innovative ideas. This concept fascinated Rohit, and he continued thinking of it even amidst his school and tuition classes.

As he delved deeper into the entrepreneurship world Rohit discovered related terms like 'innovation' and 'entrepreneurship'. The more he learned, the more he found it interesting and exciting. Recognising his enthusiasm, Rohit's parents supported his newfound interest and enrolled him in online courses. Over the next three to four years, Rohit mastered various business topics, including app and web development.

The First Startup Begins

After years of learning and honing his skills, Rohit felt the need to put his knowledge to practical use. On his birthday in 2018, he launched his first startup–a firm specialising in application, web development, and robotics. However, starting a venture at such a young age came with its own challenges.

Rohit encountered obstacles like registering the firm and setting up an account while dealing with the limitations imposed by his minor age. Nevertheless, he persisted and managed to overcome these hurdles, gradually expanding the firm from a micro-scale operation to a small-scale venture. With each step forward, Rohit's determination grew stronger.

Rising Above the Pandemic

In 2020, the world was hit by the COVID-19 pandemic, leading to widespread lockdowns and economic uncertainty. While many businesses struggled to survive, Rohit refused to let it deter him. He saw it as an opportunity to further push his skills and knowledge.

Undeterred by the losses incurred during the pandemic, Rohit launched a new platform in 2021. This community-based platform provided students and developers with a space to learn, assess their skills, and build technical knowledge. Rohit assembled a team and trained over 1,000 students in the first month itself. The platform quickly gained momentum and garnered recognition from various esteemed organisations, including the governments of America, India, and Australia.

Recognition and Appreciation

Rohit's dedication and achievements did not go unnoticed. The government, along with various public and private organisations, recognised his hard work. His firm secured a place in the top 100 startup challenges multiple times, furthering its reputation.

The turning point came when Rohit was invited to present his innovative startup at Indian Union Territory of Puducherry in the presence of its Hon'ble Chief Minister and the Lieutenant Governor. These wins fuelled Rohit's determination. Moreover, the Hon'ble Governor of Jharkhand recognised his outstanding contributions.

Rohit also showcased his startup at the National Technology Day event in Delhi and received accolades from the Prime Minister. The recognition and appreciation received from both government and non-government organisations served as a catalyst, inspiring Rohit to work efficiently and effectively.

Balancing Success and Education

Despite his remarkable achievements in the entrepreneurial world, Rohit remained grounded and single-mindedly dedicated to his education. Once an ordinary student, he steadily improved his academic performance. By the time he reached grades 11 and 12, Rohit had become the go-to person for sharing study notes and clearing doubts, both for his classmates and his juniors, especially in subjects like Innovation, Entrepreneurship and Computer Science.

Rohit's consistent hard work as an entrepreneur and his dedication to education earned him the respect and reverence of his peers and teachers. He believed that education provided a solid foundation for his entrepreneurial endeavours, playing a vital role in his future.

Expanding Horizons

With his firms gaining momentum and making a significant impact, Rohit decided it was time to expand his horizons. He ventured into the field of strained intelligence and machine learning, recognising their potential to revolutionise industries.

Rohit started collaborating with field experts and attended workshops and conferences to improve his knowledge. He implemented AI and ML techniques in various projects, including developing smart solutions for healthcare and agriculture. His work garnered interest both in India and abroad, earning him invitations to speak at global conferences and share his insights.

Paying It Forward

Rohit strongly believed in the power of giving back to society and helping aspiring entrepreneurs. He aimed at mentoring and guiding young individuals with entrepreneurial goals. Through a program, he shared his experiences, provided resources, and motivated budding entrepreneurs to pursue their dreams fearlessly.

Rohit initiated many philanthropic activities, supporting causes such as education for underprivileged children and environmental conservation. He understood the responsibility that came with success and used his position to create a positive impact in the world.

Future Endeavours

As Rohit's journey continued, he remained focussed on pushing the boundaries and creating a lasting impact. He now plans to establish an innovation hub that brings together bright minds from different fields to interact and work on cutting-edge solutions for global challenges.

Rohit dreams of revolutionising education by bridging the gap between traditional learning and practical skills required in the modern world. He envisions a future where every student has access to quality education and the opportunity to explore their potential.

With his unwavering determination, passion for innovation, and dedication to making a difference, Rohit's journey from a dream to a reality is far from over. He continues to inspire and empower individuals to pursue their passions and contribute to the society.

Whether you're a recent graduate, a student exploring entrepreneurial possibilities, or someone seeking a new direction in your career, *School to Startup: Navigating the Path of Entrepreneurship* is your roadmap to success. Get ready to embark on an exciting adventure where you'll unleash your potential, create something remarkable, and make your mark in the world. Let's undertake this transformative journey together!

Part - 1

PREPARING FOR THE JOURNEY

The Power of an Entrepreneurial Mindset
Unleash Your Inner Potential

Have you ever considered the remarkable power that lies within you, waiting to be unleashed? It's the power of an entrepreneurial mindset–one that empowers you to think boldly, embrace innovation, and create your own path to success. By developing this mindset, you can tap into your inner potential and embark on a journey of entrepreneurship that will not only transform your life but also impact the world. Let's explore this incredible power of an entrepreneurial mindset and discover how it can shape your destiny.

Embracing an entrepreneurial mindset enables one to see the world through a variegated lens. It takes challenges as opportunities, risks as potential rewards, and setbacks as valuable learning experiences. This mindset lets you think outside the box, question the status quo, and envision new possibilities. It empowers you to counter conventional thinking and find innovative solutions to complex problems. With an entrepreneurial mindset, you will be the maker of your own destiny, forging a path uniquely yours.

One of the most powerful aspects of an entrepreneurial mindset is its ability to fuel your creativity and give momentum to innovation. It encourages you to explore uncharted territories, discover independence from the limitations of conformity, and unleash your imagination. By embracing this mindset, you can bring about change, constantly seeking ways to improve and innovate. It's through the power of creativity and innovation that unbridled ideas are born and transformed into reality.

An entrepreneurial mindset is not immune to failure or setbacks. In fact, it embraces them as essential components of the journey to success. With this mindset, failure becomes a stepping stone rather than an obstacle. It teaches you resilience, the ability to bounce back stronger and wiser. Instead of fearing failure, you embrace it as an opportunity for growth and learning. You understand that each setback brings valuable lessons that propel you forward on your entrepreneurial path.

Another incredible power of an entrepreneurial mindset is its ability to foster a sense of empowerment and self-belief. It ignites the fire within you, giving you the conviction to pursue your dreams and overcome challenges. With this belief, you recognise that you have the power to create your own opportunities, to shape your own future, and to leave a lasting legacy. You navigate your own ship through uncertain waters with unwavering determination and faith in your abilities.

An entrepreneurial mindset further encourages collaboration and the power of networking. It recognises that success is not achieved in isolation but through the joint efforts of a supportive community. You learn to connect with like-minded individuals, build strong relationships, and leverage the strengths of others. You understand that collaboration and networking strengthen your impact and open doors to new possibilities.

In conclusion, the power of an entrepreneurial mindset is immense. It empowers you to think differently, to embrace innovation, and to take action. With this mindset, you unleash your inner potential and embark on a journey of self-discovery and transformation. It equips you with the tools to navigate challenges, overcome setbacks, and create your own path to success. Develop the power of an entrepreneurial mindset and realise your full potential. The world is waiting for your unique contributions, your innovative ideas, and your entrepreneurial spirit. Adopt this approach, and there will be no limit to what you can achieve.

1.1 Understanding Entrepreneurship: Embrace Your Journey of Innovation and Impact

Have you ever longed to create something meaningful to make a difference in the world? If yes, then you are on the right path to understanding entrepreneurship–a journey that involves adopting the spirit of innovation, identifying opportunities, and transforming ideas into reality. By immersing yourself in the essence of entrepreneurship, you can unlock your potential and begin a life-changing journey of impact and fulfilment.

To truly understand entrepreneurship, you must recognise that it goes beyond merely starting a business. It is about becoming an innovator, a disruptor, and a visionary. It is the art of identifying gaps in the market, finding ground-breaking solutions, and taking calculated risks to bring those ideas to life. With an entrepreneurial temperament, you open yourself up to a world of possibilities, where you have the power to shape industries and create positive change.

As you delve deeper into the realm of entrepreneurship, you will discover the fundamental principles that lead to successful ventures. You will learn to identify opportunities where others see challenges and envision a future that others have yet to imagine. This ability to see beyond the surface sets entrepreneurs apart. They develop a keen eye for recognising unmet needs and a relentless effort to meet those needs through innovative solutions. One needs to open up to possibilities and grow a curious mind that seeks new ways to solve problems and make a meaningful impact.

Entrepreneurship is not a solitary endeavour. It thrives on collaboration, networking, and forging connections. Surround yourself with like-minded individuals who share your passion for ideation and innovation. Engage in conversations, seek mentorship, and learn from those who have already walked the path before you. Identify the power of collaboration and teamwork, for it is through shared experiences and diverse perspectives that ground-breaking ideas are born.

In the world of entrepreneurship, failure is not a roadblock but a stepping stone to success. Know that failure is not an indication of your worth or abilities, but an opportunity to learn and grow. Learn lessons from setbacks and use them to modify your strategies and approaches. The most successful entrepreneurs have experienced their fair share of failures, but their resilience and determination keep them afloat. Remember, each failure brings you one step closer to success.

By understanding entrepreneurship, you can have a strong impact on society. As an entrepreneur, you have the power to create positive change, to solve pressing societal issues, and to change and improve others' lives. Shoulder this responsibility with humility and empathy. Seek to build ventures that not only generate profit but contribute to the greater good. Lace your entrepreneurial skills with moral values and strive to create a sustainable and socially responsible enterprise.

In conclusion, understanding entrepreneurship is a journey

of self-discovery, innovation, and impact. It requires developing the mindset of an innovator, recognising opportunities amidst challenges, and learning from failures. It is all about building connections, collaborating with others, and bringing a positive change in the world. Start this journey with passion and purpose, and unlock your potential as an entrepreneur. The world is waiting for your ideas, your innovation, and your impact. Embrace entrepreneurship and embark on a transformative path of personal and professional growth.

1.2 Cultivating an Entrepreneurial Mindset: Unleashing Your Inner Innovator

Have you ever felt a deep desire to carve out your own path and create something extraordinary? It's time to cultivate an entrepreneurial mindset—a way of thinking that empowers you to innovate, take calculated risks, and be a pioneer in the field. By cultivating this mindset, you can tap into your full potential and get on a transformative journey of entrepreneurship. Let's explore how you can nurture an entrepreneurial mindset and unleash your creative prowess.

Cultivating an entrepreneurial mindset begins with opening up to possibilities and accepting change. It's all about challenging the status quo, questioning conventional wisdom, and daring to dream big. Instead of getting bogged down by limitations, you see every obstacle as an opportunity for growth and innovation. You recognise that change is the only constant that acts as an impetus for progress. By shifting your perspective and approach, you create a fertile ground fit for entrepreneurial thinking to thrive.

One of the key pillars of cultivating an entrepreneurial mindset is developing a passion for learning and continuous growth. Recognise that knowledge is power and that every failure holds new lessons. It encourages you to seek information, acquire new skills, and expand your horizons. With lifelong learning, you stay ahead of the curve, adapt to unfavourable circumstances, and unlock new opportunities.

Risk-taking is another significant quality required to grow an entrepreneurial mindset. It requires stepping out of your comfort zone and venturing into the unknown. While risks can be intimidating, an entrepreneurial mindset empowers you to assess and manage them effectively. It encourages calculated risks, where you weigh the potential rewards versus the pitfalls. By taking risks, you open yourself up to new possibilities and make room for growth and innovation.

Resilience is a fundamental trait of an entrepreneur. It is the ability to bounce back from setbacks, learn from failures, and persist during adversities. Resilience involves reframing failure as a learning opportunity and accepting it as a stepping stone to success. With an entrepreneurial mindset, you understand that setbacks are temporary and that perseverance is the key to achieving goals.

An entrepreneurial mindset thrives on curiosity and an undying thirst for exploration. It encourages you to ask questions, counter assumptions, and seek innovative solutions. Curiosity fosters a spirit of discovery and openness to new ideas. You discover untapped opportunities, make connections, and find innovative solutions to difficult problems.

Collaboration and networking are vital components of cultivating an entrepreneurial mindset. They foster a sense of belonging and exposure to diverse perspectives and expertise. By embracing collaboration, you tap into the shared knowledge of others, leverage their strengths, and create cooperative relationships. This mindset encourages you to build a supportive network of like-minded individuals who can provide guidance, inspiration, and opportunities for collaboration.

In conclusion, cultivating an entrepreneurial mindset is a transformative journey that empowers you to think innovatively, embrace risk, and unleash your full creative potential. It involves shifting your perspective, adapting to change, and nurturing characteristics such as lifelong learning, resilience, curiosity, and networking. By cultivating this mindset, you open yourself up to a world of possibilities, where you can create meaningful and lasting impact. Exude the power of an entrepreneurial mindset, and embark on a journey of self-discovery, innovation, and growth. The world is waiting for your entrepreneurial spirit to shine.

1.3 Overcoming the Fear of Failure: Embrace Your Journey of Growth and Success

Have you ever been tied down by a paralysing fear holding you back from pursuing your dreams? Fear of failure can be a formidable speed breaker that prevents us from taking risks, exploring new opportunities, and realising our full potential. However, it's time to rise above this fear and see failure not as an endpoint but as a stepping stone on the path to success. By overcoming the fear of failure, you open yourself up to a world of growth, resilience, and unparalleled achievements. Let's explore how you can conquer this fear and begin your journey towards growth and success.

The first step in overcoming the fear of failure is to reframe your perspective. Rather than viewing failure as a reflection of your worth or abilities, see it as a crucial part of the learning process. Recognise that failure is not the denial of success but its vital component. Failure provides valuable lessons, insights, and growth opportunities. Believe that every setback puts learning, adjusting, and improving at stake.

Another powerful way to overcome the fear of failure is to

shift your focus from outcomes to effort. Instead of worrying about the potential negative consequences of failure, channel your energy into giving your best. Trust the process, celebrate your small wins on the way, and know that your hard work and dedication will bring you closer to your goals. By shifting your focus from outcomes to effort, you can distance yourself from the fear of failure and bring yourself to focus on the present moment.

Embracing a growth mindset is instrumental in overcoming the fear of failure. Your skills and intelligence can bloom only through dedication and hard work. Understand that failure is not a reflection of your capabilities but an opportunity for growth. Take challenges as chances to test your abilities, learn new skills, and become a better version of yourself. With a growth mindset, you transform failure into a building block for personal and professional growth.

It's essential to surround yourself with a supportive network of like-minded individuals who understand and fathom the entrepreneurial journey. Find mentors and peers who have experienced failures and setbacks but have risen beyond them. Engage in conversations, share your fears and aspirations, and learn from their experiences. Their guidance and support will help you navigate the challenges of entrepreneurship and give you the conviction to overcome the fear of failure.

Taking calculated risks is an integral part of entrepreneurship. Instead of succumbing to the fear of failure, take calculated risks. Evaluate the potential rewards and consequences of your actions and make informed decisions. Taking calculated risks is essential for growth and success. By stepping outside your comfort zone, you expand your horizons, gain valuable experiences, and unlock new opportunities.

Lastly, practice self-compassion and resilience. Treat

yourself with kindness and understanding, recognising that failure does not reflect your worth as a person. Cultivate resilience by bouncing back from setbacks, learning from mistakes, and persevering in the face of challenges. With each failure, remind yourself that you have the strength and resilience to rise and chase your dreams.

In conclusion, overcoming the fear of failure is a transformative journey that requires a shift in perspective, adopting a growth mindset, surrounding yourself with a supportive network, taking calculated risks, and cultivating resilience. By reframing failure as an opportunity for growth, you break free from the shackles of fear and open doors to success. Take challenges, venture into the unknown, and pick up valuable lessons that failure brings. With every failure, you move one step closer to realising your dreams and making a profound impact on the world. Start the journey of overcoming the fear of failure and unlock your true potential.

1.4 Embracing Creativity and Innovation: Unleash Your Widespread Potential

Have you marvelled at the positive creativity that stems from the widespread power of human imagination? Creativity and innovation are the driving forces that foster progress and change. It's time to unlock your own creative potential and embrace a mindset that leads to innovation. By embracing creativity and innovation, you open yourself up to a world of innumerable possibilities where you can make a lasting impact and bring your wildest ideas to life. Let's explore how to cultivate this mindset and unleash your inner creative genius.

The first step in embracing creativity and innovation is to think outside the box. Discover freedom from conventional thinking and push the limiting boundaries. Embrace a mindset that encourages curiosity and open-mindedness. Explore new ideas, perspectives, and approaches. Let your imagination run wild and see where it leads you. Give yourself the freedom to think differently and create a fertile ground for innovative ideas.

Creating an environment that nurtures creativity is crucial. Surround yourself with things that inspire and stimulate your imagination. Seek diverse experiences, engage in new hobbies, and absorb different cultures and perspectives. Don't shy away from experimenting and taking risks. Accept failures as valuable learning opportunities. Remember that some of the greatest innovations stem from the willingness to take risks and learn from setbacks.

An essential quality for being creative and innovative is continuous learning. Feed your mind with knowledge from various domains, as diverse ideas often collate to form groundbreaking innovations. Explore opportunities to expand your skills and knowledge through workshops, courses, and reading. Consider learning as a lifelong journey that holds the potential to give birth to a new idea or insight.

Collaboration is another key factor in fostering creativity and innovation. Recognise the power of shared knowledge and the different viewpoints that come from collaborating with others. Surround yourself with a diverse network of individuals who can question your thinking, inspire new ideas, and provide valuable feedback. Engage in brainstorming sessions, team projects, and collaborations that encourage an exchange of ideas. By embracing collaboration, you tap into the joint wisdom of a team and leverage the strengths of others to bring your ideas to fruition.

Accepting failure is instrumental in fostering creativity and innovation. Failure is not a setback but an integral part of the creative process. Every failure brings you closer to success by providing valuable insights and lessons. Learn from your mistakes, change your approach, and persevere when faced with challenges. By taking failure as a stepping stone to success, you give an impetus to innovative thinking.

Finally, allow yourself to play and have fun. Foster a childlike curiosity and sense of wonder. Engage in activities that ignite your passion and bring you joy. Playfulness and a light-hearted approach can fuel your creativity and open doors to innovative ideas. Explore and experiment without the pressure of immediate results. Remember, some of the most ground-breaking innovations have come from the most unexpected and playful ideas.

In conclusion, developing creativity and innovation is a transformative journey that involves granting yourself the freedom to think differently, creating a nurturing environment for creativity, fostering continuous learning, encouraging collaboration, accepting failure, and permitting yourself to have fun. By embracing these principles, you tap into your extensive potential and unlock the power of your imagination. Revel in the joy of creating, let your ideas soar, and leave your unique mark on the world through your creative and innovative endeavours. The world eagerly awaits the magic you have to offer.

Identifying Your Passion and Purpose
Unleashing Your True Potential

Have you ever thought of the deeper meaning of your existence? The quest for passion and purpose is an integral part of the human experience. It's time to embark on a journey of self-discovery, discover your interests, strengths, and values, and identify the true passions that ignite your soul. By aligning your passions with a meaningful purpose, you can unlock your full potential and create the life that you desire. Let's find out how to identify your passion and purpose and set the stage for a fulfilling and purpose-driven journey.

The first step in identifying your passion and purpose is to explore your interests and curiosity. Think of the activities that make your heart sing and bring you immense joy. What subjects, hobbies, or experiences drive you and fuel your enthusiasm? Engage in a variety of activities, from arts and sports to volunteering and learning new skills. Be mindful of the moments when you lose track of time and try to stay immersed in the present. These are the clues that can lead you to your true passions.

Self-reflection is a powerful tool in the pursuit of passion and purpose. Take the time to delve deep within yourself and understand your personal values and beliefs. What matters the most to you? What do you stand for? Identify the values that guide your actions and decisions. Reflect on the kind of impact you want to make in the world and the causes that ignite your passion. By aligning your passions with your values, you create a powerful force that drives your purpose.

Another essential factor in identifying your passion and purpose is recognising your unique strengths and talents. Reflect on your innate capabilities and the things that come easily to you bringing you a sense of accomplishment. Consider the skills and knowledge you have. What are you exceptionally good at? How can you use your strengths to make a meaningful contribution? By understanding your unique gifts, you can align them with your passions to create a purpose-driven life.

What impact do you want to have on others and the world? What problems do you feel compelled to solve? How do you want to make a difference? Consider the issues that stir your emotions and spark a sense of urgency within you. Identify the areas where you can channel your passions to create positive change. By aligning your passions with a higher purpose, you tap into a sense of fulfilment and meaning that goes beyond personal gratification.

Experimentation and exploration are key components for finding your passion and purpose. Don't be wary of trying new things and stepping outside your comfort zone. Engage in diverse experiences, meet new people, and expose yourself to different cultures and perspectives. Embrace the mindset of continuous growth and learning. Through experimentation, you can gain valuable insights into what truly resonates with you and what ignites your passion.

Remember, identifying your passion and purpose is not easy. It's a dynamic and evolving process that requires patience and self-compassion. Give yourself the freedom to explore different paths and take detours that may lead you to unexpected discoveries. Trust your intuition and follow the inner voice that guides you towards your true calling.

In conclusion, identifying your passion and purpose is strictly a personal and transformative journey. By exploring your interests, reflecting on your values, recognising your strengths, understanding the impact you want to make, and experimenting, you set the stage for a life filled with passion and purpose. Embark on self-discovery, for within you lies the ability to unleash your true potential and live a life full of contentment. Identify your passions, follow your purpose, and embark on the journey of a purpose-driven life.

2.1 Exploring Your Interests and Strengths: Unleashing Your Full Potential

Have you ever wondered what truly makes you come alive? The key to unlocking your full potential is understanding your unique interests and strengths. By exploring these, you can uncover latent talents, passions, and possibilities that can shape a fulfilling and purposeful life. It's time to embark on a journey of self-discovery, where you delve into your interests and strengths and unleash your full potential. Let's explore how you can embark on this transformative journey.

To begin, take a moment to reflect on your interests. What activities, subjects, or hobbies grab your attention? Think of all the things that bring you joy, excitement, and a sense of fulfilment. Consider the moments when you feel most productive and engaged. Whether it's a particular sport, originative pursuit, or intellectual pursuit, your interests hold clues to your passions. Explore various areas of interest and see where your imagination takes you.

As you explore your interests, focus on the latent strengths and talents that come naturally to you. Reflect on the activities where you excel and the skills that set you apart. Your strengths are the building blocks of your potential. They represent your unique gifts and skills that, when nurtured and developed, can lead to unparalleled achievements. Take note of your strengths, whether they lie in problem-solving, communication, creativity, leadership, or other areas. Recognise and embrace them as the foundation for unleashing your full potential.

It is essential to introspect during this exploration process. Set aside time to ponder over and solve your problems. Consider the moments when you feel energised, in flow, and fully engaged. These moments often reveal a connection between your interests and strengths. Reflect on the tasks or projects that you find particularly rewarding and fulfilling. Ask yourself why they resonate with you. Understanding the reasons behind your passions can guide you towards a path that aligns with your true self.

Engaging in new experiences is a powerful way to expand your interests and discover new strengths. Step outside your comfort zone and explore activities outside of your usual realm. Take up new hobbies, enrol in courses, or join clubs and organisations that align with your curiosities. By exposing yourself to diverse experiences, you broaden your perspective and open doors to new interests and talents. Be a lifelong learner, constantly seeking opportunities to grow and discover new passions.

As you explore your interests and strengths, remember that it is your journey. Avoid comparing yourself to others or conforming to societal expectations. Embrace your individuality and honour your true self. Your interests and strengths are the building blocks of your personal growth and success. Embrace them fully, without judgement or hesitation, and bask in the glory of the diverse qualities that make you who you are.

By exploring your interests and strengths, you discover the path to a life filled with passion and purpose. As you tap into your innate talents and pursue activities that ignite your curiosity, you are filled with a sense of fulfilment and joy. Embark on the journey of self-discovery, for within it lies the key to unleashing your full potential. Feel free to explore, embrace your strengths courageously, and discover the innumerable possibilities. The world eagerly awaits your unique gifts and talents.

2.2 Finding Your True Passion: Unleashing the Fire Within

Have you ever yearned to discover that one thing that sets your soul on fire? The pursuit of passion is a journey of self-exploration, a quest to discover the activities, causes, or endeavours that bring you immense joy, fulfilment, and purpose. It's time to embark on a transformative journey, where you dive deep into your desires, dreams, and curiosities to find your true passion. Let's explore how to embark on this exhilarating quest and unleash the fire within.

Finding your true passion begins with self-awareness. Take the time to reflect on your desires, dreams, and aspirations. What activities make you feel productive and fully alive? What are the things you would do just for the sheer joy of doing them? Look for the moments in your life when you feel a deep sense of fulfilment and contentment. These glimpses offer insightful clues to your passions. Embrace your desires without judgement or limitations, for they hold the keys to unlocking your true potential.

Discover your natural talents and strengths as you embark on this journey of self-discovery. Reflect on your natural latent talents and skills. What are the things you effortlessly excel at? Notice where you receive accolades and recognition from others. Your talents are like hidden gems waiting to be discovered. By embracing and developing these innate abilities, you can direct them towards your true passion and create a powerful impact.

Step outside your comfort zone and explore a wide range of experiences. Be open to trying new things, engaging in different activities, and venturing into uncharted territories. Embrace the unknown with wonder and courage. By exposing yourself to diverse experiences, you expand your horizons and gain a deeper understanding of yourself. It brings you closer to your true passion, whether by confirming your indispensable coalition with the field or guiding you toward unexpected avenues.

Pay attention to the things that ignite a sense of purpose and meaning within you. What causes or issues resonate with your heart? Consider the problems you feel compelled to solve or the areas where you want to make a difference. Finding your true passion often involves aligning it with a purpose of personal fulfilment. By connecting your passion with a greater cause, you tap into motivation and inspiration that propels you forward.

Develop a curious mindset as you navigate the path to finding your true passion. Cultivate a thirst for knowledge and continuous learning. Explore different subjects, engage in conversations with experts, and immerse yourself in the wealth of information available. As you gather insights and expand your understanding, you may discover new areas of interest or unexpected connections that fuel your passion.

Remember, the journey to finding your true passion is not constantly linear. It may involve twists and turns, moments of doubt, and periods of exploration. Embrace the process with patience and resilience. Allow yourself to go with the flow and change as you gain new insights and self-awareness. Your true passion may evolve, and that is perfectly natural. Trust your inner capabilities, listen to your intuition, and have faith that the path beyond will unfold.

In conclusion, finding your true passion is a transformative journey of self-discovery. Through self-awareness, exploring your talents, undergoing new experiences, finding a sense of purpose, and maintaining curiosity, you can unleash the fire within and create a life filled with passion and fulfilment. Open up to adventure, venture into the unknown, and embrace the limitless potential within you. Your true passion awaits, ready to ignite your spirit and propel you towards a life of purpose and joy.

2.3 Aligning Your Passion with Purpose: Igniting a Life of Meaning and Fulfilment

Have you ever longed to live a life filled with purpose and meaning? The key to unlocking a fulfilling and impactful life lies in aligning your passion with purpose. When your passion and purpose come together, their powerful collaboration guides you towards a path that not only brings you joy but also makes a positive difference in the world. It's time to embark on a transformative journey of self-discovery, where you align your passion with purpose and ignite a life of meaning and fulfilment.

To begin, take a moment to reflect on your passions. What activities, causes, or endeavours bring you immense joy, excitement, and a sense of fulfilment? What ignites a fire within you and makes you come alive? Feel free to explore your passions without limitations or judgement. Your passions fuel your way towards a purposeful life. Embrace them fully, for they hold the key to unlocking your unique contribution to the world.

Once you have identified your passions, it is essential to connect them with a sense of purpose. Reflect on the impact you want to make in the world, the change you wish to see, and the values you hold dear. Consider the causes or issues that resonate with your heart and align with your passions. Ask yourself how your passions can be channelled to serve a greater purpose and personal fulfilment. When you connect your passion with purpose, you tap into motivation and inspiration that fuels your journey.

As you embark on the path of aligning your passion with purpose, it is important to be self-aware. Take the time to explore your values, strengths, and unique talents. Reflect on the qualities that set you free and your natural skills. Your unique skills are the tools you can leverage to make a meaningful impact. By recognising and developing these talents, you prove your worthiness to align your passion with purpose and create a positive ripple effect in the world.

Engage in self-reflection and introspection to gain clarity on your purpose. Ask yourself profound questions such as: What legacy do I want to leave behind? How do I want to contribute to the well-being of others and the world at large? What mark do I want to make during my time on this planet? By diving deep into these inquiries, you can discover the essence of your purpose and infuse it into your passion.

Remember that aligning your passion with purpose is not a destination but a continuous journey. Your purpose may evolve as you gain new insights and experiences. Trust the process with wide-eyed wonder and an open mind. Allow yourself the freedom to explore and adapt as you discover new layers of your passion and purpose. Stay true to your values, listen to your intuition, and believe in finding the path ahead.

In conclusion, aligning your passion with purpose is a transformative endeavour that leads to a life of fulfilment, meaning, and impact. By identifying your passions, connecting them with a sense of purpose, and cultivating self-awareness, you can ignite a fire within you that propels you towards a purposeful life. Embrace the journey, for within it lies the opportunity to make a positive difference in the world and leave your unique mark. Align your passion with purpose and unleash the limitless potential within you. The world eagerly awaits your contribution.

Developing Essential Skills for Success
Unleashing Your Full Potential

Have you wondered what sets successful individuals apart? Extensive innate talent and luck, it is the particular set of essential skills that propels individuals towards success in various domains of life. By cultivating these skills, you can unlock your full potential and navigate the challenges and opportunities that come your way. It's time to embark on a transformative journey of self-improvement, where you develop essential skills for success and unleash the limitless capabilities within.

3.1 Constructive Liaison and Networking: Unlocking Opportunities for Success

Have you wondered how some individuals effortlessly navigate social interactions, build strong relationships, and seize opportunities? The secret lies in their mastery of constructive liaison and networking skills. These skills not only enable you to express yourself with clarity and impact but also empower you to connect with others openly and build a valuable network. By honing your networking abilities, you can unlock a world of opportunities and walk towards success.

Effective communication is a cornerstone of personal and professional success. It is the art of expressing your thoughts, ideas, and emotions in a well-spoken and convincing manner that keeps the listener interested. To develop your communication skills, start by practicing active listening. Focus on truly understanding what others are saying, ask thoughtful questions, and provide feedback that demonstrates your engagement. Express yourself with clarity, using concise and well-structured messages. Pay attention to your language, tone of voice, and non-verbal cues, as they profoundly influence how your message is received.

Along with listening and speaking clearly, effective communication involves adapting your style to suit your audiences and contexts. Consider the needs, preferences, and communication styles of those you interact with, and carve your way accordingly. Whether you are communicating with colleagues, clients, or friends, strive to build rapport and create an environment of trust and mutual understanding. By mastering constructive communication, you improve your ability to express your ideas, resolve conflicts, influence others, and build strong relationships.

Networking is an essential skill that opens doors to opportunities and expands your sphere of influence. Networking is not only about collecting business cards or making superficial connections; it is about forging true connections based on mutual respect and shared interests. Start by seeking networking opportunities, whether through professional events, industry conferences, or online platforms. Engage in conversations, show genuine interest in others, and find global ground to establish meaningful connections.

To build a strong network, it is important to offer value and support to others. Be generous with your time, knowledge, and resources. Offer assistance, share insights, and connect with people who may benefit from each other's expertise. The more you contribute to the success of others, the stronger your network becomes. Remember, networking is a two-way street. Embrace the mindset of reciprocity, and be open to receiving support and guidance.

Maintaining and nurturing your network requires constant effort and care. Stay in touch with your connections through regular communication, such as emails, phone calls, or meetings. Seek opportunities to collaborate, share experiences, and celebrate successes together. By investing time and energy in your network, you foster a supportive union that can provide invaluable advice, mentorship, and new opportunities.

Effective communication and networking go hand in hand. When you communicate effectively, you create connections that form the foundation of your network. Your network provides you with a platform to enhance your communication skills. By engaging in diverse conversations, you broaden your perspectives, polish your communication style, and develop the ability to adapt to wider audiences.

In conclusion, constructive communication and networking are essential skills that empower you to unlock opportunities and success. By mastering the art of communication, you can express yourself with clarity and impact, build strong relationships, and resolve conflicts effectively. Simultaneously, networking allows you to connect with like-minded individuals, cultivate pure relationships, and acquire new opportunities. Embrace the journey of developing these skills, for they will serve as the keys to unlocking your full potential and creating a successful and fulfilling life.

3.2 Leadership and Team Building: Unleashing the Joint Potential

Do you see yourself as a leader who inspires others, drives change, and achieves remarkable results? Leadership is not rising to a title or position; it is a mindset and a set of skills that can be cultivated. By developing your leadership skills and mastering the art of team building, you can unleash the joint potential of a group and succeed in limitless achievements. Get ready to embark on a journey of leadership and team building, where you ignite inspiration, foster collaboration, and lead others towards success.

Leadership is much more than just giving orders or making decisions; it is about guiding and inspiring others to unlock a worldwide vision. To become a constructive leader, start by being self-aware. Understand your strengths, weaknesses, values, and motivations. By knowing yourself, you can lead with authenticity and integrity, aligning your stance with your principles. Embrace continuous learning and personal growth, seeking feedback and reflecting on your experiences to polish your leadership skills.

Empathy and emotional intelligence are crucial aspects of leadership. Develop the ability to understand and connect with others on a deeper level. Practice active listening, show genuine interest in others' opinions, and demonstrate empathy and understanding. By fostering an inclusive and supportive environment, you encourage collaboration, uplift morale, and create a sense of belonging within your team.

Effective communication is a hallmark of successful leadership. As a leader, you must be worldly-wise to express your vision, goals, and expectations clearly. Communicate with transparency and authenticity, sharing information openly and encouraging open dialogue. Ensure that your team members feel heard and understood, and provide timely and constructive feedback to facilitate their growth and development.

Team building is an indispensable quality of leadership, as a strong team is the foundation of any successful endeavour. Start by recruiting individuals who complement each other's strengths and skills, fostering a diverse and well-rounded team. Create a shared purpose and an articulate set of goals that align with the larger vision. Nurture a culture of trust, collaboration, and accountability, where team members feel safe to express their ideas and take calculated risks.

As a leader, it is essential to empower your team members and provide them with the resources and support they need to succeed. Assign tasks effectively, matching them to individual strengths and particular areas. Encourage creativity and innovation, permitting team members to explore new ideas and approaches. Foster a learning environment where mistakes are viewed as opportunities for growth, and celebrate both individual and joint achievements.

To build a high-performing team, lead by example. Demonstrate integrity, professionalism, and a strong work ethic. Inspire and motivate your team through your actions, embodying the values and behaviours you expect from them. Recognise and laud their contributions, fostering a positive and supportive work culture that encourages collaboration and continuous improvement.

Effective leadership and team building require resilience and flexibility. As a leader, you must be willing to navigate challenges and embrace change. Encourage a growth mindset within your team, where individuals are open to learning, unafraid of failure, and willing to embrace new opportunities. Create a culture that fosters innovation and continuous learning, where team members feel free to share their ideas and experiment with new approaches.

In conclusion, leadership and team building are essential skills that enable you to unleash the joint potential of a group and achieve remarkable results. By cultivating self-awareness, empathy, constructive communication, and a growth mindset, you can inspire others, foster collaboration, and guide your team towards success. Embrace the journey of leadership and team building, for within it lies the power to create positive change and make a lasting impact on those around you.

3.3 Problem Solving and Visualisation Making: Empowering Yourself to Navigate Challenges

Have you ever faced a complex problem or found yourself struggling to make a crucial decision? In today's fast-paced and ever-changing world, the ability to powerfully solve problems and make sound decisions is a valuable skill that can set you apart. By developing your problem-solving and decision-making abilities, you empower yourself to navigate challenges, seize opportunities, and achieve your goals. Get ready to embark on a journey of critical thinking, creativity, and rational decision-making.

Problem-solving is the process of identifying, analysing, and resolving obstacles or issues that hinder progress. To become a constructive problem solver, start by developing a proactive mindset. Embrace challenges as opportunities for growth and learning, rather than viewing them as huge obstacles. Develop curiosity and a thirst for knowledge, seeking to understand the root causes of problems rather than merely addressing the symptoms.

Critical thinking is crucial in problem-solving. Turn complex issues into manageable parts and gather relevant information through research, data analysis, and seeking input from others. Look at the problem from multiple perspectives, exploring different angles and considering various potential solutions. Embrace creativity and out-of-the-box thinking, as it can lead to innovative and constructive solutions.

Once you have gathered information and generated potential solutions, it is time to evaluate their feasibility and potential outcomes. Consider the advantages and disadvantages of each option, weighing the risks and benefits. Use alert thinking to assess the potential impact on different stakeholders and the broader context. It is also essential to consider future implications and long-term consequences. By adopting a systematic and rational approach to problem-solving, you increase the chances of finding practical solutions.

Decision-making is closely intertwined with problem-solving. Making sound decisions involves assessing information, considering alternatives, and choosing the interests that align with your goals and values. To enhance your decision-making skills, start by clarifying your objectives and identifying the desired outcome. This will serve as a guiding light in evaluating different options.

When faced with a decision, gather relevant information and consider both qualitative and quantitative factors. Seek input from trusted advisors or experts who can provide valuable insights and perspectives. Engage in thoughtful reflection, weighing the potential risks and rewards associated with each option. It can be helpful to use decision-making frameworks, such as SWOT or cost-benefit analysis, to guide your evaluation.

While it is important to make informed decisions, it is equally crucial to embrace the element of uncertainty. Not all decisions have transparent answers or predictable outcomes. It takes courage to make decisions in difficult or uncertain situations. Trust your decision, listen to your intuition, and be willing to learn from both successes and failures. Remember, decision-making is a continuous process, and adjustments can be made on the way if necessary.

Effective problem-solving and decision-making involve constructive communication and collaboration. Engage with stakeholders, seek their input, and build consensus. Embrace diverse perspectives, as they can enrich your understanding of the problem and broaden the range of potential solutions. Foster a culture that encourages open dialogue, respect for different opinions, and constructive feedback.

In conclusion, problem-solving and decision-making are essential skills that empower you to navigate challenges and make informed choices. By raising a critical mindset, embracing creativity, and applying rational thinking, you can tackle complex problems with confidence. Combine these skills with constructive communication, collaboration, and a willingness to learn from both successes and failures. Embrace the journey of problem-solving and visualisation for within it lies the power to overcome obstacles, seize opportunities, and achieve your goals.

3.4 Flexibility and Resilience: Thriving in an Ever-Changing World

Have you been in a situation where circumstances changed unexpectedly, and you had to quickly retreat and find a way forward? In today's dynamic and unpredictable world, the ability to change and overcome challenges is a valuable skill that can make all the difference. By developing your flexibility and resilience, you empower yourself to navigate uncertainty, embrace change, and thrive in the face of adversity. Get ready to embark on a journey of flexibility, growth, and unwavering determination.

Adaptability is the ability to adjust to new situations, environments, and demands. It requires a mindset of openness, curiosity, and a willingness to learn. By staying informed and constantly acquiring new knowledge, you position yourself to navigate changes effectively.

To cultivate adaptability, start by embracing a growth mindset. Believe that your talents and skills are not fixed, rather they can be polished and honed over time. Take challenges as opportunities for growth and learning, rather than obstacles to overcome. Develop a sense of marvel and a willingness to explore new ideas and approaches. This mindset allows you to see change as an opportunity for personal and professional development.

Flexibility is another key quality of adaptability. Be open to new ideas and perspectives, and be willing to step outside your comfort zone. Embrace uncertainty and be comfortable with ambiguity. This allows you to respond quickly and powerfully when faced with unexpected situations. Emphasise agility and the ability to switch and turn when necessary, adjusting your strategies and plans to align with changing circumstances.

Resilience is the ability to bounce back when faced with setbacks, adjust to adversities, and maintain a positive attitude amidst challenges. It is an essential skill in a world where obstacles and failures are inevitable. Resilience allows you to persevere, learn from setbacks, and keep moving forward towards your goals.

To develop resilience, start by building a strong support network. Surround yourself with people who uplift and encourage you during difficult times. Seek guidance from mentors or trusted friends who can provide opinion and support. Cultivate self-care practices that nurture your physical, emotional, and mental well-being. This includes getting rest, engaging in activities that bring you joy, and practicing mindfulness or meditation to build emotional resilience.

Developing a positive mindset is also crucial in building resilience. Focus on the things you can control rather than dwelling on those you can't. Embrace challenges as opportunities for growth and view setbacks as learning experiences. Practice gratitude and cultivate optimism, finding the silver linings amidst adversity. This positive mindset fuels your resilience and gives you the strength to persevere.

Adaptability and resilience are not just individual traits; they also extend to your interaction with others. Collaboration and teamwork are essential in navigating changes and overcoming challenges. Embrace diversity and value different perspectives, as they can offer new insights and solutions. Foster a culture of open communication, trust, and empathy within teams and organisations. Encourage mutual support and a shared sense of purpose, as it strengthens flexibility and resilience.

In conclusion, flexibility and resilience are vital skills that enable you to thrive in an ever-changing world. By cultivating an open mindset, embracing flexibility, and developing resilience, you empower yourself to navigate uncertainty, overcome obstacles, and seize new opportunities. Embrace the journey of resilience, for within it lies the power to not only survive but also to thrive during change.

Building a Solid Foundation
Setting Yourself Up for Success

Are you ready to embark on an exciting journey of entrepreneurship and build your own startup? Before you dive headfirst into the world of innovation and business, it is essential to lay a solid foundation. Just as a sturdy structure requires a strong base, your startup needs a solid foundation to thrive and succeed. By focusing on key elements such as market research, business planning, funding, and legal considerations, you can set yourself up for success. Get ready to build a solid foundation that will support your entrepreneurial dreams.

4.1 Conducting Market Research: Unleashing the Power of Insights

Are you ready to launch your startup and make a meaningful impact in the marketplace? Before you take that leap, it's crucial to understand the importance of conducting market research. Market research is the process of gathering and analysing information about your target market, customers, competitors, and industry trends. By probing deep into the intricacies of the market, you can uncover valuable insights that will shape your business strategies, product development, and marketing efforts. Get ready to embark on a journey of discovery where you unleash the power of market research.

The first step in conducting market research is understanding your target market. Who are your potential customers? What are their demographics, behaviours, preferences, and needs? By identifying your target market, you can tailor your products or services to meet their specific requirements and develop constructive marketing strategies to reach them. Use surveys, questionnaires, interviews, and focus groups to gather data and gain insights into their motivations, pain points, and purchasing behaviours. The more you understand your target market, the better equipped you'll be to serve them.

Competitive examination is another crucial component of market research. Study your competitors to gain a deep understanding of their strengths, weaknesses, strategies, and market positioning. Know their products or services, pricing, distribution channels, marketing campaigns, and consumer feedback. By understanding the competitive landscape, you can identify gaps and opportunities in the market and differentiate yourself from the competition. This knowledge will guide your product development, pricing strategies, and marketing efforts, giving you a competitive edge.

Market research also allows you to stay informed about industry trends and emerging market opportunities. Monitor industry publications, news sources, and industry-specific websites to stay updated with the latest developments. Follow trade shows, conferences, and networking events to connect with industry professionals and gain valuable insights. By staying informed about industry trends, you can identify potential shifts, new technologies, or emerging markets that may impact your business. This knowledge will enable you to change your strategies and seize new opportunities as they arise.

The methods and tools for conducting market research have grown with the advancement of technology. Online surveys, social media listings, and web analytics provide valuable data and consumer insights. Leveraging these digital tools to collect quantitative and qualitative data will inform your decision-making. Check online reviews, social media discussions, and consumer feedback to understand consumer psychology and identify areas for improvement. Use data analytics tools to track website traffic, user behaviour, and conversions. The digital landscape offers a wealth of information waiting to be discovered.

Market research is not a one-time concern, but an ongoing process. Continuously monitor and evaluate your market to stay ahead of evolving trends and changing consumer preferences. Regularly gather customer feedback, track your key performance indicators, and review market dynamics to assess the effectiveness of your strategies. This continuous process allows you to fine-tune your approach, make informed decisions, and optimise your business for success.

In conclusion, conducting market research is a significant step in launching and growing your startup. By understanding your target market, studying your competitors, staying informed about industry trends, and leveraging digital tools, you gain invaluable insights that shape your business strategies and lead you towards success. Market research empowers you to make data-driven decisions, mitigate risks, and seize opportunities in the marketplace. Embrace the power of market research, for within it lies the knowledge and understanding that will fuel your entrepreneurial journey.

4.2 Crafting a Compelling Business Plan: Your Roadmap to Success

Are you ready to turn your entrepreneurial vision into a reality? Devising a compelling business plan is a crucial step on your journey to startup success. A business plan serves as your roadmap, outlining your objectives, strategies, and financial projections. It is not only a tool to secure funding or investors but also a strategy that guides your decision-making and provides the right direction for your startup. Get ready to dive into the world of business planning and craft a compelling roadmap that will lead you to success.

The first step in crafting a compelling business plan is defining your vision and mission. What is the purpose of your startup? What problems are you solving or needs are you fulfilling? Clearly express your vision and mission, capturing the essence of your venture. This sets the tone for your business plan and helps stakeholders understand your purpose and goals.

Next, thoroughly analyse your target market. Who are your potential customers? What are their needs, preferences, and behaviours? Understanding your target market enables you to tailor your products or services to meet their specific demands. Research market trends, identify potential opportunities, and know the competitive landscape. By demonstrating a deep understanding of the market, you show potential investors or partners that you have a solid foundation for success.

One of the most crucial sections of your business plan is the introduction of your products or services. Clearly explain what you offer and how it solves a problem or fulfils a need. Highlight the unique features and benefits that set your product or service apart from the competition. Include any intellectual property or proprietary technology that gives you a competitive advantage. This section demonstrates the value proposition of your startup and convinces stakeholders of its market potential.

Your business plan should also outline your marketing and sales strategies. How will you reach your target market? What channels and tactics will you use to promote your offerings? Develop a comprehensive marketing plan that covers online and offline strategies, branding, pricing, distribution, and consumer acquisition. Your marketing and sales strategies should align with your target market and differentiate your startup from competitors.

Financial forecasts are an integral part of a convincing business plan. Develop realistic financial forecasts that project your revenue, expenses, and profitability over a specific period. Include details on your pricing model, forfeit structure, sales estimates, and cash flow analysis. This section demonstrates the financial viability of your startup and assures investors that you have a plan to generate returns on their investment.

A carefully-thought business plan also includes an organisational structure and an overview of your team. Define the roles and responsibilities within your startup, highlighting the skills and expertise of key team members. Show that you have a strong and capable team in place to execute your strategies and boost the success of your startup. Additionally, outline your future hiring plans, demonstrating your growth strategy and scalability.

Lastly, revise and refine your business plan. Seek feedback from mentors, advisors, or industry experts to ensure its clarity and effectiveness. Polish your writing, check for grammatical errors, and ensure that your plan is easy to read and understand. A well-presented and professionally written business plan instils conviction in stakeholders and shows that you are serious about your venture.

In conclusion, crafting a compelling business plan is a crucial step in your entrepreneurial journey. By defining your vision and mission, conducting market analysis, describing your products or services, outlining marketing and sales strategies, estimating finances, and showcasing your team, you create a roadmap to success. Your business plan serves as a powerful tool that guides your decision-making, attracts investors, and aligns your team with your vision. Embrace the process of crafting a compelling business plan, for within it lies the road ahead for your startup's success.

4.3 Securing Funding and Resources: Unlocking the Path to Startup Success

Are you ready to take your startup to the next level? Securing funding and resources are crucial steps in transforming your entrepreneurial dreams into reality. Whether you want to develop your product, expand your operations, or scale your business, acquiring the necessary funding and resources is essential for growth and success. Get ready to embark on a journey of financial planning, strategic partnerships, and resource acquisition that will unlock the path to startup success.

The first step in securing funding and resources is developing a comprehensive financial plan. Take the time to assess your startup's financial needs and create a detailed plan that outlines your expenses, revenue estimates, and predictable cash flow. This financial plan will serve as a roadmap to guide your fundraising efforts and demonstrate to potential investors or lenders that you have an articulated understanding of your financial requirements.

One of the primary sources of funding for startups is external investment. This can come from kind investors, venture capitalists, or crowdfunding platforms. Research and identify potential investors who align with your industry and investment criteria. Prepare a compelling pitch deck that highlights the value proposition of your startup, market potential, competitive advantage, and financial forecasts. Present an articulate plan for how the investment will be utilised to boost growth and generate returns for the investors.

In addition to external investment, securing grants or government funding can provide a significant uplift to your startup. Research for grants and programs that cater to startups in your industry or geographical location. Develop a compelling grant proposal that outlines how your startup aligns with the objectives of the grant and how the funds will be utilised to reach specific milestones. Government funding agencies and organisations often have specific criteria and processes, so be sure to thoughtfully follow their guidelines.

Strategic partnerships can also be instrumental in securing resources for your startup. Interact with established companies or organisations that can provide access to expertise, technology, distribution channels, or other valuable resources. Seek out partnerships that align with your goals and can offer mutual benefits. The right strategic partnership can not only provide access to resources but also lend credit and validation to your startup.

Don't overlook the power of bootstrapping and self-funding as well. Utilise your own savings, personal loans, or credit cards to fund your startup in the early stages. This demonstrates your dedication to your venture and reduces the dependency on external funding sources. Bootstrapping also encourages a lean and resourceful mindset, forcing you to be creative and efficient in utilising the resources available to you.

Networking and building relationships in your industry can open doors to funding and resources. Follow industry events, conferences, and networking meetups to connect with potential investors, mentors, and industry experts. Join startup accelerators or incubators that provide access to funding, mentorship, and a supportive network of entrepreneurs. Leverage these relationships to gain insights, advice, and potential introductions to investors or resource providers.

Lastly, prepare a compelling business specimen and pitch that highlights the potential return on investment for potential funders or resource providers. Clearly explain the market opportunity, competitive advantage, growth potential, and your startup's unique value proposition. Demonstrate that you have a solid plan for utilising the funds or resources to boost growth, generate revenue, and attach value to your target market.

In conclusion, securing funding and resources is a critical step in the success of your startup. By developing a comprehensive financial plan, seeking external investment, exploring grants and government funding, establishing strategic partnerships, networking, and leveraging self-funding, you can unlock the resources needed to fuel your growth. Be persistent, strategic, and expressive in your fundraising efforts, and constantly be prepared to change your plan of action based on the feedback and opportunities that arise. With the right funding and resources, you can accelerate the growth of your startup and unlock its full potential.

4.4 Establishing Legal and Financial Structures: Safeguarding Your Startup's Success

Congratulations on taking the leap into entrepreneurship! As you embark on your startup journey, one crucial quality to consider is establishing solid legal and financial structures. Setting up the right legal and financial framework is essential for protecting your business, complying with regulations, managing risks, and ensuring long-term success. Get ready to navigate the world of legal and financial considerations and establish the foundation that will safeguard your startup's future.

The first step in establishing legal and financial structures is to determine the legal entity for your startup. Will you operate as a sole proprietorship, partnership, limited liability visitor (LLC), or corporation? Each entity type has its own advantages and disadvantages, so it's important to weigh factors such as liability protection, taxation, governance, and scalability. Seek translating from a legal professional to determine the most suitable legal structure for your startup's needs.

Once you've chosen a legal structure, it's time to register your business with the government authorities. Obtain the necessary licenses, permits, and registrations required to operate legally in your industry and jurisdiction. This step ensures compliance with local laws and regulations and prevents potential legal issues down the lane. It's important to stay informed about any ongoing compliance requirements and make sure your business remains in good standing with the relevant authorities.

Next, consider the importance of protecting your intellectual property (IP). Intellectual property includes trademarks, copyrights, patents, and trade secrets that are unique to your startup's offerings. File trademark applications to protect your trademark identity and logo, and copyright your original creative works. If your startup involves proprietary technology or inventions, consult with an expert to explore the possibility of filing for patents. Safeguarding your IP resources is crucial for maintaining a competitive whet and preventing unauthorised use or infringement.

Financial management is another critical quality of establishing strong foundations for your startup. Open a separate business account to have your personal and business finances separate. This helps maintain well-judged financial records, simplifies tax filing, and protects your personal resources in case of legal issues. Implement written systems and software to track income, expenses, and cash flow. Consider hiring a bookkeeper to ensure well-judged financial reporting and compliance with tax regulations.

In addition to financial management, it's important to establish proper financial controls and processes. Implement a robust bookkeeping system, maintain organised financial records, and establish articulate financial policies and procedures. This ensures transparency, accountability, and mitigates the risk of fraud or financial mismanagement. Regularly review and resolve your financial statements to gain insights into the financial health of your startup and make informed business decisions.

Another key consideration in establishing legal and financial structures is managing risks and securing unobjectionable insurance coverage. Identify potential risks and liabilities associated with your startup's activities, and explore apt insurance options to protect against those risks. This may include unstipulated liability insurance, professional liability insurance, product liability insurance, or property insurance. Consult with an insurance professional to assess your specific needs and find the right coverage for your startup.

Finally, seek legal counsel to monitor or review contracts, agreements, and other legal documents that are essential to your startup's operations. These may include consumer contracts, vendor agreements, employment contracts, non-disclosure agreements (NDAs), and partnership agreements. A well-drafted contract can protect your rights, define responsibilities, and mitigate potential disputes.

In conclusion, establishing legal and financial structures is a crucial step in safeguarding your startup's success. By choosing the right legal entity, registering your business, protecting your intellectual property, implementing sound financial management practices, managing risks, and securing apt insurance coverage, you lay a solid foundation for growth and protect your business from potential legal and financial pitfalls. Seek guidance from legal and financial professionals to ensure compliance with regulations and practices. With the right legal and financial structures in place, you can focus on building your startup with confidence, knowing that you have taken the necessary steps to protect your business and its assets. These structures provide a framework for your operations, establish clear guidelines, and help you navigate the complex landscape of legal and financial obligations.

Part - 2

TAKING THE LEAP

Launching Your Startup
Turning Vision into Reality

Congratulations on reaching a significant milestone in your entrepreneurial journey–the launch of your startup! This is an exciting time filled with anticipation, energy, and innumerable possibilities. As you prepare to introduce your product or service to the world, it's essential to direct the launch with careful planning and strategic execution. In this chapter, we will explore the key steps involved in launching your startup and guide you through this transformative process.

5.1 Defining Your Unique Value Proposition: Standing Out in a Crowded Market

Congratulations on taking the first steps toward launching your startup! As you embark on this exciting journey, one of the most critical tasks you'll face is defining your unique value proposition. Your value proposition sets you apart from competitors and communicates the unique benefits and value your product or service offers. It is the foundation upon which you will build your brand, entice customers, and boost business growth. In this chapter, we will explore the importance of defining your unique value proposition and guide you through the process of crafting a compelling statement that resonates with your target audience.

To begin, it's crucial to have a deep understanding of your target market. Who are your loyal customers? What are their needs, pain points, and desires? Go through market research and gather insights to gain an articulate understanding of your target audience. This will help you identify gaps in the market and discover opportunities to differentiate yourself.

Next, know your product or service and identify its unique features and benefits. What makes it special? How does it solve a problem or fulfil a need better than existing solutions? Consider the specific attributes, functionalities, or innovations that set your offering apart. This could include superior quality, cost-effectiveness, convenience, speed, customisation, or an unparalleled consumer experience.

Once you have a clear understanding of your target market and the unique aspects of your product or service, it's time to craft your value proposition statement. Start by defining the benefits or values you are offering to your customers. This should be a brief and compelling statement that captures the essence of your value proposition. Keep it simple, memorable, and customer-focused.

When drafting your value proposition statement, consider these key elements:

- Target Audience: Clearly define the specific regulars or consumer segment you are targeting. This helps tailor your message to resonate with their needs and preferences.
- Differentiation: Highlight the unique aspects of your product or service that distinguish it from competitors. Emphasise what makes you stand out in the market.

- Benefit: Communicate the primary benefit customers will gain by choosing your offering. Focus on the value it provides and how it solves their problem or fulfils their desire.
- Proof: Support your value proposition with vestige or proof points that validate your claims. This could include consumer testimonials, case studies, or data-driven results.

Remember to keep your value proposition customer-centric. Focus on how your product or service addresses the pain points or challenges faced by your target customer. It should clearly demonstrate the value customers will receive by choosing your offering over other alternatives.

Once you have drafted your value proposition statement, test it with your target audience. Seek feedback, conduct surveys, or perform A/B testing to gauge its effectiveness. Refine and repeat as necessary to ensure your value proposition resonates with your customers and powerfully communicates your unique advantages.

Your unique value proposition should permeate throughout all aspects of your business, from marketing materials to sales pitches. Continuously communicate your value proposition across various channels, including your website, social media, advertisements, and consumer interactions. This helps build a strong brand identity and creates a lasting impression in the minds of your customers.

In conclusion, defining your unique value proposition is a significant step in differentiating your startup in a crowded market. By understanding your target audience, identifying your unique features and benefits, and crafting a compelling value proposition statement, you position yourself to entice and retain customers. Keep refining and evolving your value proposition as your business grows and market dynamics change. With an articulate and compelling value proposition, you are well-equipped to stand out, make a meaningful impact, and boost the success of your startup.

5.2 Developing a Minimum Viable Product (MVP): Testing the Waters of Innovation

Congratulations on reaching the stage of developing your startup's product or service! As you embark on this crucial phase, it's important to embrace the concept of a Minimum Viable Product (MVP). The MVP is a strategic channel that allows you to test your ideas, gather valuable feedback, and validate your assumptions while minimising risks and costs. In this chapter, we will explore the significance of developing an MVP and guide you through the process of creating a compelling and constructive version of your product or service.

First and foremost, it's essential to understand the concept of an MVP. An MVP is the most simplified version of your product or service that provides value to your target audience. It is not meant to be a fully-featured or polished final product but rather a functional prototype that demonstrates your concept. By focusing on the essential features and functionalities, you can bring your idea to life quickly and efficiently.

The concept of an MVP serves multiple purposes. Firstly, it allows you to test your assumptions and hypotheses about your target market, consumer needs, and product-market fit. By putting your MVP in the hands of potential customers, you can gather feedback and know whether your solution solves their problem effectively. This early feedback is invaluable in shaping your product strategy and ensuring you are on the right track.

Developing an MVP also helps you manage risks and costs. By developing a scaled-down version of your product or service, you can save time and resources that would have been spent on developing unnecessary or unproven features. This allows you to reflect and switch quickly based on consumer feedback, unforeseen mistakes or wasted efforts.

To develop an effective MVP, start by identifying the features and functionalities that align with your value proposition and write the key pain points of your target audience. Focus on delivering a solution that solves a specific problem or meets a particular need, rather than trying to create a comprehensive solution from the outset. This way, you can launch quickly and start gathering feedback as early as possible.

Once you have identified the key features, it's time to prioritise and build your MVP. Keep in mind that the goal is to make a functional and usable version of your product. The focus should be on functionality rather than aesthetics. It's important to strike a balance between delivering value and keeping the process practical and efficient.

Consider leveraging existing tools, frameworks, or platforms to improve the functionality of your MVP. This could involve using third-party services, open-source software, or leveraging cloud-based solutions to minimise the need for extensive coding or infrastructure setup. The key is to focus on speed and agility in getting your MVP into the hands of potential users.

Once your MVP is developed, it's time to launch and gather feedback from your target audience. Encourage users to provide their thoughts, suggestions, and insights on their experience with your product or service. Collect the data and feedback you receive to identify areas for improvement. This iterative process allows you to refine and enhance your product based on real-world user feedback.

It's important to keep in mind that an MVP is not a one-time effort but rather an ongoing process. As you receive feedback and gather insights, repeatedly enhance your product or service based on user needs and preferences. Continuously seek feedback, note user behaviour, and change your MVP accordingly. This ensures that you are constantly refining and evolving your offering to deliver maximum value to your target audience.

In conclusion, developing a Minimum Viable Product (MVP) is a crucial step in the startup journey. By focusing on essential features, gathering user feedback, and improvising based on real-world insights, you can validate your assumptions, mitigate risks, and refine your product or service.

5.3 Building an Effective Team: Harnessing Joint Power for Startup Success

Congratulations on reaching the stage of building your startup team! As you embark on this adventure, it's crucial to understand the importance of forming an effective and cohesive team. A strong team is the crux of any successful startup, as it brings together diverse talents, skills, and perspectives to boost innovation and reach shared goals. In this chapter, we will explore the key principles and strategies for building an effective team that can propel your startup to new heights.

The first step in building a constructive team is to define the roles and responsibilities needed to realise your startup's objectives. Identify the key areas of expertise required, such as technology development, marketing, sales, finance, and operations. Consider the specific skills, experience, and personalities that would complement your strengths and fill any gaps in knowledge or expertise. By clearly defining roles and responsibilities, you set the foundation for a well-structured and functional team.

When selecting team members, look for individuals who not only possess the necessary skills and qualifications but also align with your startup's values, vision, and culture. Seek out individuals who are passionate, driven, and share your entrepreneurial mindset. Cultural fit is essential for fostering a collaborative and harmonious working environment where team members can thrive and contribute their best.

Diversity is another crucial element to consider when building your team. Seek individuals with different backgrounds, perspectives, and experiences. A diverse team brings a broader range of ideas, creativity, and problem-solving approaches. It fosters innovation and helps you tap into different market segments and consumer preferences. Embrace diversity in all its forms, including gender, ethnicity, age, and educational background, as it contributes to a rich and dynamic team.

Once you have formed your team, it's important to encourage open and constructive communication. Encourage open dialogue, active listening, and sharing of ideas and feedback. Create a culture where team members feel valued in expressing their opinions and challenging the status quo. Constructive networking ensures that everyone is aligned, working towards common goals, and enlightened of progress.

As a leader, your role is to provide guidance, support, and motivation to your team members. Lead by example and demonstrate the qualities and behaviour you expect from your team. Foster a positive and inclusive work environment where team members feel valued, empowered, and motivated to give their best. Encourage a culture of continuous learning and personal growth, and provide opportunities for skill and career advancement.

Teamwork and collaboration are essential for harnessing the

joint power of your team. Encourage collaboration and cross-functional cooperation, where team members can leverage their individual strengths and skills to reach shared objectives. Foster a sense of belonging and mutual support, where team members are willing to help one another and celebrate each other's successes. Promote a culture of trust, transparency, and accountability, where everyone takes ownership of their responsibilities and delivers on their commitments.

Regularly assess the dynamics and performance of your team. Provide constructive feedback and support individual growth and development. Identify any conflicts or issues early on and write them promptly and constructively. Strive for continuous resurgence and seek opportunities to enhance team effectiveness and cohesion.

In conclusion, building a constructive team is a crucial component of startup success. By assembling a diverse and talented team, fostering open communication, providing constructive leadership, promoting teamwork and collaboration, and nurturing a positive work culture, you can harness the joint power of your team and boost innovation and growth. Remember, your team is the engine that will propel your startup forward, so invest time and effort in building a team that will set the stage for success.

5.4 Setting Up Operations and Infrastructure: Building the Foundation for Startup Success

Congratulations on reaching the stage of setting up operations and infrastructure for your startup! As you embark on this crucial phase, it's important to understand the significance of establishing a solid foundation that supports the smooth functioning of your business. Constructive operations and infrastructure lay the groundwork for efficiency, scalability, and long-term success. In this chapter, we will explore the key considerations and strategies for setting up operations and infrastructure that will take your startup forward.

The first step in setting up operations and infrastructure is to define your business processes. Take the time to identify the individual activities and tasks that are essential for delivering your product or service. Map out the workflows–from procurement to production, from marketing to consumer service. Streamline and optimise these processes to eliminate inefficiencies and enhance productivity. This will ensure that your startup operates systematically and efficiently.

Next, consider the technology and tools required to support your operations. Invest in reliable and scalable technology solutions that align with your business needs and goals. This may include software for project management, consumer relationship management (CRM), inventory management, or accounting. Leverage cloud-based solutions that offer flexibility, accessibility, and data security. Implement a robust IT infrastructure to support your business operations, including hardware, software, and network infrastructure.

Physical infrastructure is equally important in setting up operations. Evaluate your space requirements and identify the apt location for your startup. Consider factors such as accessibility, proximity to suppliers or customers, and potential for expansion. If your business requires manufacturing or warehousing facilities, ensure that the space is unobjectionable and optimised for efficient operations. Pay attention to safety and security measures to protect your resources and ensure the well-being of your team.

Human resources are a vital component of your startup's infrastructure. Rent the right talent that aligns with your business objectives and culture. Clearly define job roles and responsibilities, and provide thorough on boarding and training to new employees. Foster a positive work environment that encourages collaboration, learning, and growth. Develop articulate policies and procedures to guide employee conduct, performance, and benefits. By investing in your human resources, you build a strong foundation for your startup's success.

Developing strong relationships with suppliers and vendors is another significant quality of setting up operations and infrastructure. Identify reliable and trustworthy partners who can provide the necessary resources, materials, or services to support your business. Negotiate contracts and terms to ensure the timely delivery of goods or services. Maintain open networking lines and establish healthy relationships with your suppliers and vendors.

Quality is essential to ensure your products or services meet or exceed consumer expectations. Implement rigorous quality check procedures to monitor and assess the quality of your offerings. Regularly review and refine these processes to ensure continuous quality delivery and consumer satisfaction. Establish feedback mechanisms to gather consumer insights and use that feedback to improve products or services.

As your startup grows, consider the scalability of your operations and infrastructure. Anticipate future growth and plan to cater to increased demand. Make your operations flexible to adapt to changing market conditions or consumer needs. Continually evaluate and optimise your processes, systems, and resources to support scalability and maintain a competitive edge.

In conclusion, setting up operations and infrastructure is a crucial step in building the foundation for your startup's success. By defining your business processes, leveraging technology, establishing physical infrastructure, investing in human resources, forging supplier relationships, ensuring quality control, and planning for scalability, you create a solid framework that supports the efficient and constructive functioning of your business. With a strong operational foundation, you can focus on growing your startup and achieving your long-term goals.

Marketing and Branding Strategies
Building a Strong Market Presence

Welcome to the exciting world of marketing and branding! As you embark on your entrepreneurial journey, it's crucial to understand the power of effective marketing and branding strategies in shaping the success of your startup. In this chapter, we will explore the key considerations and strategies for developing a strong marketing presence and building a compelling brand that resonates with your target audience.

6.1 Understanding Your Target Audience: Unlocking the Key to Successful Marketing

Welcome to the world of marketing, where understanding your target consumer is the foundation of success. As an entrepreneur, it's crucial to grasp the importance of knowing your potential consumers inside out to powerfully reach, engage, and convert them into loyal customers. In this chapter, we will explore the significance of understanding your target audience and discover strategies to gain valuable insights into their needs, preferences, and behaviours.

To begin, let's focus on the fundamental concept of a target audience. Your target audience is the specific group of people who are most likely to be interested in your product or service. They are the individuals who have a genuine need or desire for what you offer. Identifying and understanding your target audience allows you to tailor your marketing efforts and create a convincing message that resonates with them.

The first step in understanding your target audience is conducting thorough market research. This process involves gathering data and insights about your potential customers, their characteristics, motivations, and pain points. Start by defining your target market based on demographics such as age, gender, location, occupation, and income level. These demographic factors provide a deep understanding of who your potential customers are.

Apart from demographics, it's essential to dive deeper into psychographics, which include attitudes, values, beliefs, and lifestyle preferences. Psychographic information helps you understand your audience's motivations, interests, and behaviours, allowing you to connect with them on a deeper level. Conduct surveys, interviews, and focus groups to gather qualitative data and gain insights into their desires, challenges, and aspirations.

Another valuable tool for understanding your target audience is creating beneficiary personas. A beneficiary persona is a fictional representation of your potential customer. It combines demographic and psychographic information to create a detailed profile of your target audience. Give your persona a name, age, occupation, and personal background. Identify their goals, challenges, and decision-making factors. This persona becomes a reference point to guide your marketing strategies and ensure your communication is tailored to their specific needs.

Once you have an articulate understanding of your target audience, you can develop targeted messaging that speaks directly to them. Craft a value proposition that addresses their pain points and showcases how your product or service solves their problems or fulfils their desires. Use language, tone, and imagery that resonates with their preferences and aligns with their values. By speaking their language, you establish a connection and build trust.

Effective networking with your target audience requires selecting the right marketing channels. Identify the platforms and channels where your audience spends their time and engage with them. This could be social media platforms like Facebook, Instagram, LinkedIn, or industry-specific forums and communities. Be present on these channels, share relevant content, and urgently engage with your audience. This not only helps you reach your target audience but also allows you to listen to their feedback, understand their concerns, and refine your marketing strategies.

Continuous monitoring and analysis of your target audience's interests and preferences are essential for adapting your marketing efforts. Use web analytics tools to track website traffic, user behaviour, and conversion rates. Monitor social media metrics to gauge engagement and identify trends. Get consumer feedback, reviews, and surveys to gather insights and make informed decisions. Stay updated with changes in your target audience's needs and preferences, and adapt your marketing strategies accordingly.

In conclusion, understanding your target audience is the cornerstone of successful marketing. By conducting thorough market research, creating beneficiary personas, tailoring your communication, selecting the right channels, and continuously analysing consumer behaviour, you gain valuable insights that inform your marketing strategies. Remember, the better you understand your target audience, the better you can connect with them, build strong relationships, and boost your startup's success.

6.2 Creating a Strong Brand Identity: Unleashing the Power of Your Unique Identity

Welcome to the world of branding, where creating a strong brand identity is the key to standing out in a crowded marketplace. As an entrepreneur, developing a unique and compelling brand identity is crucial for establishing a strong presence, building consumer loyalty, and driving the success of your startup. In this chapter, we will explore the significance of creating a strong brand identity and discover strategies to help you define and communicate your brand effectively.

To begin, let's understand the importance of brand identity. Your brand identity is the unique combination of elements that distinguishes your brand from competitors and makes it memorable to your target audience. It goes beyond just a logo or a tagline. It includes your brand's values, personality, mission, and visual elements, all working together to create a cohesive and pure representation of your business.

The first step in creating a strong brand identity is defining your brand's values and personality. Ask yourself: What does your brand stand for? What are the principles and beliefs that guide your business? Define the characteristics that you want your brand to stand for, whether it's innovation, trustworthiness, or creativity. These values and personality traits will serve as the foundation of your brand identity.

Next, consider the visual elements that will represent your brand. This includes your logo, colour palette, typography, and imagery. Each of these elements should be thoughtfully chosen to align with your brand's values and personality. For example, vibrant colours and playful fonts might be suitable for a brand targeting a younger audience, while muted colours and elegant typography might be apt for a luxury brand. Ensure consistency in the use of these visual elements across all your marketing materials to establish a recognisable and cohesive brand identity.

Another crucial quality of building a strong brand identity is crafting a compelling brand story. Your brand story is the narrative that communicates your brand's purpose, origins, and the value it brings to customers. Share the story behind your startup—what inspired its creation, the problem it aims to solve, and how it adds value to people's lives. Your brand story humanises your business and connects with your consumers on an emotional level, building trust and loyalty.

Consistency is key to building a strong brand identity. Ensure that your brand identity is continuously reflected in all aspects of your business—from your website and social media presence to your product packaging and consumer service. Consistency helps create a cohesive brand experience and reinforces your brand's values and personality in the minds of your audience. Establish brand guidelines that outline how your brand should be represented across different touchpoints to maintain consistency.

Effective networking is crucial for conveying your brand identity to your target audience. Draft an articulate and compelling brand message that briefly communicates what your brand stands for and the unique value it offers. Tailor your message to resonate with your target audience's needs, aspirations, and pain points. Use language and tone that aligns with your brand's personality and values. The resulting message spread across all marketing channels helps reinforce your brand identity and create a memorable impression.

Lastly, engage with your consumers and build relationships through meaningful brand experiences. Create opportunities for your target audience to interact with your brand, whether through events, social media campaigns, or social engagement. Encourage user-generated content and foster a sense of belonging virtually with your brand. These experiences create emotional connections and reinforce your brand identity in the minds of your audience.

In conclusion, creating a strong brand identity is essential for your startup's success. By defining your brand's values and personality, choosing visual elements that align with your brand, crafting a compelling brand story, maintaining consistency, and powerfully communicating your brand's message, you can establish a unique and memorable brand identity. Remember, your brand identity is not just a logo or a tagline, but a reflection of your business's essence and what sets it apart from others. It is the foundation upon which you will build your reputation and cultivate consumer loyalty. Your brand identity should resonate with your target audience, evoke positive emotions, and convey the value you offer.

6.3 Implementing Constructive Marketing Channels: Reaching Your Target Audience with Precision

Congratulations on taking the next step in growing your startup by implementing constructive marketing channels! In today's competitive business landscape, it's crucial to reach your target audience precisely and engage them through the right marketing channels. By leveraging the power of strategic marketing, you can build brand awareness, boost consumer acquisition, and ultimately propel your business towards success. In this chapter, we will explore the significance of implementing constructive marketing channels and discover strategies to help you connect with your audience meaningfully.

First and foremost, it's essential to understand your target audience inside out. Who are they? What are their demographics, interests, and behaviours? What challenges do they face, and how can your product or service provide a solution? By developing detailed beneficiary personas, you gain valuable insights that will guide your marketing efforts. With a deep understanding of your target audience, you can identify the most effective marketing channels to reach them.

One of the most powerful marketing channels today is digital marketing. The digital landscape offers a wide variety of opportunities to connect with your audience effectively. Consider implementing strategies such as search engine optimisation (SEO) to improve your website's visibility on search engines, social media marketing to engage with your audience on platforms they frequent, and content marketing to provide valuable and relevant information that establishes your expertise and builds trust. Email marketing is another constructive channel for garnering leads and staying in touch with your audience.

Social media platforms play a significant role in modern marketing strategies. Each platform has unique features and audience demographics, making it important to select the right channels for your business. Facebook, for example, has a wholesale user feature and provides full display options for targeting specific audiences. Instagram, on the other hand, is visually driven and popular among younger audiences. LinkedIn is a valuable platform for reaching professionals and establishing industry connections. Choose the platforms that align with your target audience's preferences and behaviours.

Another constructive marketing channel is content

creation. By producing high-quality and valuable content, you can excite and engage your audience. Create a visitor blog where you can share informative articles, industry insights, and expert advice. Utilise the power of video content, whether through tutorials, product demonstrations, or behind-the-scenes glimpses. Podcasts are also gaining popularity as a way to deliver valuable content and establish thought leadership. Tailor your content to the preferences of your target audience and distribute it through various channels to maximise its reach and impact.

In addition to digital marketing, traditional marketing channels also have their place in an integrated marketing strategy. Print advertising, radio, television, and mail can effectively reach specific demographics or geographic regions. Consider the unique characteristics of your target audience and evaluate whether traditional marketing channels align with your goals and budget. The key is to find the right balance between digital and traditional channels to maximise your marketing efforts.

Evaluation and analysis are crucial when implementing marketing channels. Use analytics tools to track and measure the performance of your marketing campaigns. Pay attention to key metrics such as website traffic, conversion rates, engagement levels, and consumer feedback. This data will provide valuable insights into the effectiveness of your marketing channels and help you make data-driven decisions to optimise your strategies.

Lastly, be prepared to change and evolve your marketing channels as the market and consumer behaviours change. Monitor industry trends and stay updated on emerging technologies and platforms. Keep a pulse on your target audience's preferences and modify your strategies accordingly.

By staying alert and responsive, you can constantly refine your marketing channels to ensure maximum impact and return on investment.

In conclusion, implementing effective marketing channels is crucial for reaching your target audience with precision and driving the success of your startup. By understanding your target audience, leveraging digital marketing strategies, utilising social media platforms, creating valuable content, considering traditional channels, measuring performance, and staying adaptable, you can create a comprehensive and constructive marketing plan. Remember, the key is to continuously analyse and optimise your marketing channels based on data and feedback. By staying constant to your target audience and delivering relevant and compelling messages through the right channels, you will build brand awareness, attract new customers, and foster long-term relationships. Embrace the power of marketing channels and unleash their potential to propel your startup towards success.

6.4 Building Consumer Relationships: Nurturing Connections for Long-Term Success

Congratulations on recognising the importance of building strong consumer relationships! As an entrepreneur, establishing and nurturing connections with your customers is essential for the long-term success of your startup. By building meaningful relationships, you can foster loyalty, boost your business, and gain valuable insights to modernise your products or services. In this chapter, we will explore the significance of building consumer relationships and discover strategies to help you forge lasting connections with your customers.

First and foremost, it's crucial to understand the value of customer-centricity. Putting your customers at the centre of your business ensures that their needs and preferences guide your decisions and actions. Listen actively to your customers, understand their pain points, and empathise with their challenges. By showing genuine concern, you create a foundation of trust and respect that is the cornerstone of strong consumer relationships.

Communication is the key when it comes to building consumer relationships. Establish honest and open lines of communication with your customers to foster engagement and encourage feedback. Provide multiple channels for communication, such as email, phone, social media, and live chat, to learn different preferences. Be responsive and timely in addressing consumer inquiries, concerns, and feedback. Actively seek consumer feedback and use it to improve your products, services, and overall consumer experience.

Personalisation is a powerful tool in building consumer relationships. Treat each consumer as an individual and tailor your interactions and offerings to their specific needs and preferences. Use consumer data and insights to create personalised experiences, such as personalised recommendations, special offers, or customised communication. Personalisation demonstrates that you understand and value your customers, which deepens their connection to your brand.

Consistency is crucial in building consumer relationships. Ensure that your customers have a good experience with your brand across all touchpoints, from initial contact to post-purchase interactions. Deliver on your promises and surpass consumer expectations consistently. Consistency builds trust and reliability crucial for long-lasting consumer relationships.

Building an online community for your brand is another constructive strategy for nurturing consumer relationships. Create opportunities for your customers to connect, share their experiences, and engage with your brand on a deeper level. This can be done through social media groups, online forums, events, or loyalty programs. By fostering a sense of belonging and facilitating interactions among your customers, you create a community that strengthens their loyalty to your brand.

Surprise your customers with unexpected gestures and rewards. Offer sectional perks, discounts, or freebies to show appreciation for their support. Celebrate milestones and special occasions with personalised messages or gifts. By going beyond, you create positive and memorable experiences that leave a lasting impression on your customers and reinforce their connection with your brand.

Building consumer relationships moreover involves urgently seeking feedback and resolving issues promptly. Encourage customers to provide feedback through surveys, reviews, or testimonials. Act on the feedback you receive, addressing any concerns or issues promptly. Show your customers that their opinions and satisfaction are important to you, and take steps to improve their experience continuously.

Lastly, building consumer relationships requires a long-term mindset. It's not just about selling a product or service; it's about building a mutually healthy and cherish able partnership. Focus on nurturing relationships over time, staying constant with your customers even without the initial purchase. Maintain regular communication, offer ongoing support, and keep them informed about new products, updates, or promotions. By demonstrating your concern for their success and satisfaction, you foster loyalty and create customers who are brand advocates.

In conclusion, building strong consumer relationships is a fundamental quality of business success.

By prioritising customer-centricity, fostering open communication, personalising experiences, ensuring consistency, creating a sense of community, surprising and delighting customers, seeking feedback, and raising a long-term mindset, you can forge lasting connections with your customers.

Remember that building consumer relationships is an ongoing process that requires dedication, empathy, and a genuine desire to provide value. By investing in strong consumer relationships, you lay the foundation for long-term success and create a loyal consumer base that will support and wish well for your brand. So, get started today and watch your business flourish through the power of meaningful connections with your customers.

Sales and Growth Strategies
Fuelling the Expansion of Your Startup

Welcome to the exciting world of sales and growth strategies, where the possibilities for expanding your startup are endless. As an entrepreneur, developing effective sales strategies and implementing growth-focused initiatives are essential for driving revenue, acquiring new customers, and scaling your business. In this chapter, we will explore the significance of sales and growth strategies and discover key approaches to help you reach your expansion goals.

7.1 Developing a Sales Strategy: Mapping Your Path to Success

Welcome to the realm of sales strategy, where the power to boost revenue and reach business success lies in your hands. As an entrepreneur, developing an effective sales strategy is paramount for achieving your sales goals, acquiring new customers, and building a flourishing business. In this chapter, we will explore the significance of developing a sales strategy and discover key approaches to help you map your path to success.

First and foremost, it's crucial to have an articulate understanding of your target market. Who are your loyal customers? What are their needs, pain points, and preferences? By developing beneficiary personas, you gain valuable insights to shape your sales strategy. With a deep understanding of your target market, you can tailor your channels to powerfully engage with your audience and convert them into potential customers.

A successful sales strategy starts with setting specific and measurable goals. Define your sales targets in terms of revenue, consumer acquisition, or market share. Narrow down these goals into manageable objectives and timelines. This will provide clarity and focus, enabling you to utilise resources and track progress effectively.

Segmentation is a key component of a successful sales strategy. Divide your target market into segments based on characteristics such as demographics, behaviours, or needs. By segmenting your market, you can tailor your brand message and communication channel to meet the specific needs and requirements of each segment. This personalisation increases the effectiveness of your sales efforts and enhances consumer engagement.

Once you have identified your target segments, it's time to determine the most effective sales channels to reach them. Consider both traditional and digital channels based on your target audience's preferences and behaviours. Traditional channels may include genuine sales, networking events, trade shows, or partnerships. Digital channels could consist of social media, email marketing, content marketing, and SEO. Select the channels that align with your target audience and use resources accordingly.

Sales tactics play a crucial role in executing your sales

strategy. Choose the right tactics based on your target market, product or service, and competitive landscape. These tactics may include consultative selling, relationship building, personalised communication, product demonstrations, or self-ruling trials. Adapt your tactics to meet the specific needs and pain points of your potential customers, showcasing the value your offering brings to their lives or businesses.

Apart from tactics, a strong sales team is essential for executing your sales strategy. Hire and train sales professionals with the necessary skills, knowledge, and mindset to powerfully engage with potential customers. Provide ongoing training and specific opportunities to enhance their skills and keep them up-to-date with industry trends. Foster a culture of teamwork, collaboration, and continuous revival within your sales team.

Metrics and analytics are vital for measuring the effectiveness of your sales strategy. Define key performance indicators (KPIs) that align with your sales goals, such as conversion rates, stereotype deal size, or sales trundling length. Regularly track and check these metrics to gain insights into your sales strategy performance and identify areas for improvement. Use data-driven insights to refine your approach, optimise your sales processes, and make informed decisions.

Customer relationship management (CRM) software is a valuable tool for managing and tracking your sales efforts. Implement a CRM system to centralise consumer data, track interactions, and manage sales pipelines. This enables you to streamline your sales processes, increase productivity, and enhance consumer relationship management.

Continuous learning and adapting are essential in sales strategy development. Stay informed about industry trends, market dynamics, and emerging technologies. Seek feedback from your sales team and customers to gain insights and identify areas for improvement. Embrace a culture of experimentation and modify your sales strategy based on the evolving needs and preferences of your target market.

In conclusion, developing a sales strategy is crucial for achieving your sales goals and driving business success. By understanding your target market, setting clearly defined goals, segmenting your audience, and identifying constructive sales channels, you can adapt your channels to powerfully engage potential customers. Implementing targeted sales tactics, building a strong sales team, and utilising metrics and analytics will help you measure the effectiveness of your strategy and make data-driven improvements. Embrace continuous learning to stay ahead of industry trends and evolving consumer preferences. With a well-developed sales strategy, you can confidently map your path to success, acquire new customers, and reach your business goals.

7.2 Scaling Your Startup:
Unlocking Growth and Maximising Potential

Congratulations on the success of your startup and embarking on the adventurous journey of scaling your business! Scaling is a pivotal phase that involves expanding your operations, consumer base, and revenue to unlock long-term growth and maximise your startup's potential. In this chapter, we will explore the significance of scaling your startup and discover key strategies to help you navigate this phase in your entrepreneurial journey.

First and foremost, it's crucial to lay a solid foundation for scaling. Assess the scalability of your startup model, products, and processes. Is your business model flexible enough to accommodate growth? Are your products or services scalable without compromising quality? Review your internal operations, workflows, and systems to identify any bottlenecks or areas that need optimisation. Establish a strong infrastructure that can support increased demand and enable smooth expansion.

A well-defined growth strategy is essential for scaling your startup. Set your growth objectives clearly and identify the key drivers that will propel your startup forward. Is it expanding into new markets, targeting new consumer segments, or diversifying your product offerings? Develop a comprehensive roadmap that outlines the steps, milestones, and resources required to reach your growth goals. This roadmap will serve as a guiding framework for your scaling efforts.

Building a high-performing team is important when scaling your startup. Hire talented individuals who are aligned with your vision and possess the skills and expertise necessary to boost growth. Assemble a diverse team with compatible strengths and clearly define their roles and responsibilities. Foster a culture of collaboration, continuous learning, and adaptability. Invest in training and specific programs to upskill your team and equip them with the tools they need to excel in their roles.

Investing in technology and automation can significantly streamline your scaling efforts. Leverage software solutions, cloud-based platforms, and automation tools to optimise your operations, improve efficiency, and enhance consumer experiences. Implement consumer relationship management (CRM) systems, project management tools, and analytics platforms to gain insights, track performance, and make data-driven decisions. Embrace emerging technologies that can revolutionise your industry and give you a competitive edge.

To powerfully scale your startup, focus on consumer

satisfaction and retention. Develop a deep understanding of your target market and refine your marketing strategies to reach a wider audience. Implement digital marketing tactics such as search engine optimisation (SEO), social media advertising, content marketing, and email campaigns to generate leads and boost conversions. Prioritise consumer satisfaction and invest in delivering unparalleled consumer experiences. Cultivate strong relationships with your existing customers to boost repeat business and encourage referrals.

Partnerships and collaborations can accelerate your scaling efforts. Identify strategic alliances, industry influencers, or complementary businesses that can help expand your reach and enhance your value proposition. Explore co-marketing initiatives, joint ventures, or distribution partnerships that can open new channels and access untapped markets. Collaborating with established players in your industry can provide valuable resources, expertise, and points that can fuel your growth.

As you scale, it's essential to remain flexible and adaptable. Continually monitor market trends, consumer preferences, and industry dynamics. Stay ahead of the race by embracing innovation and proactively adapting your business model, products, or strategies to meet evolving needs. Foster a culture of experimentation and learning, where failures are seen as opportunities. Regularly evaluate your scaling efforts, measure outcomes, and make necessary adjustments to stay on track.

Financial management is critical when scaling your startup. Thoughtfully manage your cash flow, and use resources strategically. Get extra funding through avenues such as venture capital, kind investors, or loans to fuel your expansion. Develop financial forecasts and models that help with scaling-related financing and revenue projections. Regularly review your financial performance and seek advice from experts or mentors to ensure financial stability and sustainability during the scaling process.

In conclusion, scaling your startup is an exciting and challenging endeavour that can unlock tremendous growth and maximise your business's potential. By laying a solid foundation, defining an articulate growth strategy, building a high-performing team, leveraging technology, focusing on consumer satisfaction and retention, forming strategic partnerships, remaining agile, and managing finances effectively, you can navigate the scaling phase successfully. Remember, scaling is not just about expanding operations; it's about optimising your processes, delivering value to your customers, and positioning your startup for long-term success. Embrace the opportunities and challenges that come with scaling, and may your journey be filled with growth and achievement.

7.3 Leveraging Technology for Growth: Unleashing the Power of Innovation

Welcome to the realm of technology-driven growth, where the possibilities are endless, and innovation is the key to unlocking your business's full potential. As an entrepreneur, leveraging technology is crucial for achieving sustainable growth, staying competitive, and maximising opportunities in the digital age. In this chapter, we will explore the significance of leveraging technology for growth and unravel key strategies to help you harness the power of innovation.

First and foremost, it's essential to understand the transformative role that technology plays in today's business landscape. Technology has revolutionised the way we communicate, collaborate, and govern our business. It has opened new avenues for reaching customers, optimising operations, and creating innovative products or services. By embracing technology, you can gain a competitive edge and position your startup for success in the digital era.

One of the primary ways technology fuels growth is by enabling efficient and streamlined operations. Automating tasks, optimising workflows, and integrating systems through technology can significantly increase productivity and reduce costs. Implement enterprise resource planning (ERP) systems, project management tools, and collaboration platforms to streamline internal processes, improve communication, and uplift overall efficiency. By leveraging technology to optimise your operations, you can focus on business activities and strategically use resources increasingly.

Digital marketing is another powerful growth driver facilitated by technology. Embrace digital channels such as social media, SEO, email marketing, and content marketing to expand your reach, engage with your target audience, and increase conversions. Leverage data analytics to gain insights into consumer behaviour, preferences, and trends, enabling you to adapt your marketing strategies for maximum impact. Personalise your message, target specific consumer segments, and measure the effectiveness of your marketing campaigns to optimise your marketing efforts and generate resulting growth.

Innovation is at the heart of leveraging technology for growth. Embrace emerging technologies and trends relevant to your industry, such as artificial intelligence (AI), machine learning, block chain, or the Internet of Things (IoT). Assess how these technologies can enhance your products, services, or processes and bring value to your customers. Invest in research and specifics to stay ahead of the curve and continuously innovate. Foster a culture of creativity, experimentation, and risk-taking within your organisation to encourage the generation of innovative ideas and solutions.

Customer experience is a critical element in driving growth, and technology can play a pivotal role in delivering unique experiences. Use technology to enhance consumer interactions, streamline purchasing processes, and provide personalised support. Implement CRM systems to centralise consumer data, track interactions, and deliver personalised experiences. Trust chatbots or virtual assistants to provide instant consumer support and improve response times. Leverage consumer feedback platforms to gather insights and make data-driven improvements to your products or services. By leveraging technology to prioritise and enhance the consumer experience, you can boost consumer loyalty, increase retention, and generate positive word-of-mouth referrals.

Collaboration and networking are essential for growth, particularly in today's interconnected world. Leverage technology to facilitate smooth networking and collaboration both within your team and with external stakeholders. Utilise project management tools, video conferencing platforms, and cloud-based document sharing to foster collaboration regardless of geographical boundaries. Embrace enterprise social networks or networking apps to encourage knowledge sharing, teamwork, and innovation within your organisation. By leveraging technology to enhance collaboration, you can harness the joint intelligence of your team and boost growth through combined effort.

Cybersecurity and data protection are crucial considerations when leveraging technology. As you opt for integrating various technologies into your business, it's important to prioritise the security of your systems, networks, and consumer data. Implement robust cybersecurity measures, including firewalls, encryption, secure data storage, and employee training on confidential practices. Regularly monitor and update your security protocols to stay ahead of potential threats.

Ensure compliance with data protection regulations and industry standards to build trust with your customers and safeguard their information. Prioritise data privacy and establish protocols for handling and storing consumer data securely.

As you leverage technology for growth, it's important to stay well-informed of emerging trends and innovations. Stay curious and continually explore new technologies that have the potential to disrupt your industry or create new opportunities. Stay constantly active with industry forums, follow conferences, and engage in networking opportunities to stay informed and build valuable relationships with like-minded entrepreneurs.

Lastly, it's crucial to have a strategic roadmap for technology adoption and integration. Evaluate your business goals and identify the technologies that align with your objectives. Develop a technology roadmap that outlines the implementation timeline, resource allocation, and expected outcomes. Prioritise investments based on their potential impact on your growth and use resources accordingly.

In conclusion, leveraging technology for growth is essential in today's digital landscape. By embracing technology, optimising operations, innovating products or services, enhancing consumer experiences, fostering collaboration, and prioritising cybersecurity, you can unlock the power of innovation and propel your startup towards sustainable growth. Embrace the opportunities technology presents, and let it be the driving factor leading your business to success.

7.4 Expanding into New Markets:
Seizing Opportunities and Broadening Your Horizons

Congratulations on considering the exciting endeavour of expanding your startup into new markets! Venturing into new territories offers tremendous potential for growth, increased revenue, and a broader consumer base. In this chapter, we will explore the significance of expanding into new markets and uncover key strategies to help you seize opportunities and successfully navigate this transformative journey.

First and foremost, it's essential to thoroughly research and understand the new markets you intend to enter. Identify markets that align with your business objectives, where there is demand for your products or services, and where you can powerfully differentiate yourself from competitors. Study the local culture, economic landscape, administrative environment, and consumer behaviours to gain insights that will shape your market entry strategy. By gathering comprehensive market intelligence, you can make informed decisions and adapt your channels to reach new markets.

Localisation is a critical quality required for expanding into new markets. Modify your products, services, and marketing strategies to cater to the specific needs, preferences, and cultural nuances of the target market. Convert your marketing materials, website, and product descriptions into the local language. Consider localising your pricing, packaging, and branding to resonate with the target audience. Contact local partners or rent local talent with a deep understanding of the market to ensure your offerings are well-received and related to the local customers.

Building strong relationships and networks in the new market is crucial for success. Establish partnerships with local distributors, retailers, or suppliers who can help you navigate the local business landscape, provide market insights, and facilitate distribution channels. Follow industry events, trade shows, and networking opportunities to connect with potential customers, partners, and key stakeholders. Engage with local business associations, chambers of commerce, or trade organisations to expand your network and gain valuable industry insights.

A robust marketing and promotional strategy is vital for gaining visibility and traction in the new market. Leverage digital marketing channels, such as social media, SEO, and online advertising, to raise awareness and generate leads. Tailor your marketing messages and campaigns to resonate with the target audience's cultural context, values, and aspirations. Engage in local PR activities, influencer collaborations, or community engagement initiatives to build brand awareness and credibility. By powerfully promoting your brand and offerings, you can grab the attention of potential customers and differentiate yourself from competitors.

In addition to marketing, consumer support plays a pivotal role in entering new markets successfully. Ensure you have a robust consumer support system to note the unique needs and challenges of the new market. Provide multilingual consumer support, either through in-house teams or outsourced services, to effectively communicate with customers and resolve any issues promptly. Use digital network channels, such as live track or social media, to provide real-time assistance and support. With strong consumer support, you can build trust, foster consumer loyalty, and differentiate your business in the new market.

Risk management is another critical consideration when expanding into new markets. Conduct a thorough risk assessment, considering political, economic, legal, and operational risks associated with the new market. Develop contingency plans and strategies to mitigate potential risks and ensure smooth business operations. Seek legal and financial advice to navigate any regulatory or compliance requirements specific to the target market. By proactively managing risks, you can protect your business interests and minimise potential setbacks.

Continuous learning and adapting are essential when entering new markets. Monitor market trends, consumer feedback, and competitive dynamics to identify opportunities for innovation and improvement. Seek feedback from local customers, partners, and stakeholders to gain insights and refine your offerings. Embrace a culture of agility, flexibility, and openness to change, permitting you to modify your strategies and tactics based on the evolving market conditions.

In conclusion, expanding into new markets is an exciting and transformative journey with immense potential for growth and success. By thoroughly researching the new markets, localising your offerings, building strong relationships, implementing constructive marketing strategies, providing unflinching consumer support, managing risks, and embracing a culture of continuous learning, you can seize the opportunities and navigate the challenges of expanding into new markets. Remember to stay adaptable, open to feedback, and responsive to the needs of the target market. With careful planning and execution, expanding into new markets can lead to significant growth, increased market share, and a broader consumer base, ultimately propelling your startup to new heights of success. So, take the leap, embrace the possibilities, and embark on the journey of expanding into new markets with conviction and determination.

Part - 3
OVERCOMING CHALLENGES AND SUSTAINING SUCCESS

Managing Risks and Failures
Turning Challenges into Opportunities

Welcome to the unpredictable world of entrepreneurship, where risks and failures are an inherent part of the journey. As an entrepreneur, managing risks and failures is crucial for sustaining and growing your business. By proactively addressing potential risks, embracing resilience, and utilising failures as learning opportunities, you can navigate the ever-changing landscape of entrepreneurship with conviction and determination. In this chapter, we will explore the significance of managing risks and failures and discover key strategies to help you powerfully handle challenges on your entrepreneurial path.

8.1 Identifying Potential Risks and Mitigation Strategies: Safeguarding Your Business's Success

Welcome to the world of entrepreneurship, where uncertainty and risk are part of the journey. As an entrepreneur, it is essential to identify potential risks that could affect your business and develop effective mitigation strategies to guarantee your success. By proactively assessing risks and implementing mitigation measures, you can minimise potential disruptions and ensure the long-term stability and growth of your business. In this chapter, we will explore the significance of identifying potential risks and learn key strategies to help you mitigate them effectively.

First and foremost, conduct a comprehensive risk assessment to identify potential threats to your business. Start by analysing the internal and external factors that could pose risks. Internal risks may include operational inefficiencies, financial vulnerabilities, or lack of proper systems and processes. External risks may arise from market volatility, technological advancements, regulatory changes, or competition. Take a holistic channel for risk assessment, considering all aspects of your business and its environment.

Once the potential risks are identified, prioritise them based on their likely occurrence and potential impact. Some risks may have a higher probability of occurrence but a lower impact, while others may have a lower probability but a higher impact. Focus on the risks that could adversely affect your business's operations, financial health, reputation, or consumer satisfaction. By prioritising risks, you can use resources and develop targeted mitigation strategies for the most critical areas.

Risk mitigation strategies should consider specific risks and minimise their impact. Here are some key strategies to consider:

- Diversification: Avoid overreliance on a single customer, supplier, or market. Diversify your consumer base, product offerings, and geographic presence to reduce vulnerability to market fluctuations or disruptions.
- Financial Planning: Maintain a solid financial foundation by implementing constructive financial management practices. Develop contingency plans, create a financial buffer, and

regularly review your cash flow to ensure you have the necessary resources to cover potential financial risks.
- Insurance Coverage: Evaluate your business's insurance needs and secure appropriate coverage. This may include unstipulated liability insurance, property insurance, professional liability insurance, or cybersecurity insurance. Work with an insurance professional to assess your potential risks and find the best coverage options.
- Cybersecurity Measures: As businesses become increasingly digital, cybersecurity risks are on the rise. Implement robust cybersecurity measures, including firewalls, encryption, secure data storage, and employee training on significant practices. Regularly update your systems and stay informed about the latest cybersecurity threats.
- Supplier and Partner Evaluation: Assess the reliability and financial stability of your suppliers and partners. Establish well-spoken contractual agreements that outline expectations, quality standards, and contingency plans in case of obstacles. Regularly review and evaluate your supplier and partner relationships to ensure they align with your business's risk mitigation goals.
- Crisis Management Planning: Develop a crisis management plan that outlines step-by-step procedures for responding to potential crises, such as natural disasters, reputational issues, or cybersecurity breaches. Identify key stakeholders, establish networking channels, and conduct regular drills to test the effectiveness of your plan.
- Regulatory Compliance: Stay informed about relevant laws and regulations that govern your industry. Develop processes and systems to ensure compliance with these regulations, reducing the risk of legal and regulatory penalties.
- Continuous Monitoring and Evaluation: Risk mitigation is an ongoing process. Regularly monitor and reassess potential risks

as your business evolves. Stay informed about industry trends, technological advancements, and market dynamics to identify emerging risks and adapt your mitigation strategies accordingly.

Remember that risk management is not about eliminating all risks; it is about identifying, assessing, and tackling them effectively. It requires a proactive and vigilant mindset, a willingness to adapt and improve. By implementing robust risk mitigation strategies, you can safeguard your business's success and ensure its long-term viability in the face of potential challenges.

In conclusion, identifying potential risks and implementing effective mitigation strategies is indispensable for safeguarding your business's success. By conducting a comprehensive risk assessment, prioritising risks, and implementing targeted mitigation measures, you can overcome potential obstacles and protect your business from adverse effects. Remember to continuously monitor and evaluate risks, change your strategies as needed, and stay informed about industry trends and regulatory changes. By taking proactive measures to manage risk, you can navigate the uncertainties of entrepreneurship with conviction and ensure long-term stability and business growth.

8.2 Learning from Failures: Embracing Growth through Resilience

Welcome to the dynamic world of entrepreneurship, where failures are not roadblocks but stepping stones to success. As an entrepreneur, you understand that setbacks and failures are an inevitable part of the journey. However, what truly matters is how you embrace and learn from these experiences to promote growth and innovation. In this chapter, we will explore the significance of learning from failures and bouncing back to become resilient and improve continuously.

First and foremost, reframe your perspective on failure. Instead of viewing it as an outcome or a personal reflection of your abilities, see failure as an opportunity for growth and learning. Understand that setbacks are inherent in the entrepreneurial journey and that the most successful entrepreneurs have faced multiple failures before reaching their goals. Adopt a growth mindset that sees failures as valuable feedback and catalysts for improvement.

One of the key aspects of learning from failures is reflection. Take the time to learn and understand what went wrong, the factors that led to the failure, and the lessons derived from the experience. Engage in honest introspection and seek feedback from others involved in the situation. Identify the specific areas where you can improve–the strategies, processes, product development, or team dynamics.

Failure should not be an endpoint but an opportunity to refine your approach. Use the insights gained from the failure to make informed adjustments and refinements in your business strategies. Embrace a consistent approach, where you continually test, evaluate, and modify your ideas, products, and processes based on feedback and real-world results. This allows you to respond quickly to changing market dynamics and consumer needs.

Feedback from customers and stakeholders is invaluable in the process of persistence. Urgently seek feedback through surveys, consumer interviews, or data analysis. Listen actively to the needs and preferences of your target audience and be open to constructive criticism. Use this feedback to refine your offerings, improve user experience, and note pain points. By involving your customers in the process, you can build stronger relationships, foster loyalty, and deliver solutions that meet their needs.

Resilience is a key symbol entrepreneurs must cultivate to navigate the challenges of failure. It is the ability to bounce back, adapt, and persevere in the face of setbacks. Cultivate resilience by maintaining a positive mindset, focusing on solutions rather than dwelling on failures. Surround yourself with a supportive network of mentors, advisors, and peers who can provide guidance, encouragement, and opinions during challenging times.

Failure should not be hidden or shamed within your organisation. Foster a culture that embraces failure as a learning opportunity. Encourage your team members to take calculated risks, experiment with new ideas, and share their experiences, both successes and failures. Create a safe space where individuals feel valued discussing failures and acquiring lessons from them. This promotes a culture of continuous learning and improvement, where failures are seen as valuable stepping stones toward success.

Learning from failures and persisting requires resilience, adaptability, and a growth mindset. Embrace failure as a natural part of the entrepreneurial journey, and commit to learning lessons from each experience. Emphasise reflection, feedback, and persistence as essential elements of your business strategy. By doing so, you can use failures to promote innovation, refine your offerings, and ultimately reach your long-term success.

In conclusion, failures should not be viewed as permanent setbacks but as opportunities for growth and improvement. By embracing failures, reflecting on their causes, and persisting based on the lessons learned, entrepreneurs can foster resilience and promote innovation. Remember that failure is not a reflection of your abilities but a necessary step towards success. With a growth mindset, a persistent approach, and an inclination towards continuous learning and improvement, you can turn failures into valuable learning experiences and propel your business forward. Embrace the challenges, setbacks, and the occasional missteps as opportunities for growth and innovation. With each failure, take the time to reflect on what went wrong and why, seeking insights and lessons that can inform your future decisions.

8.3 Developing a Growth Mindset: Unlocking Your Potential for Success

Welcome to the transformative journey of developing a growth mindset! By embracing this powerful mindset, you can unlock your full potential and achieve greater success in all areas of your life. In this chapter, we will explore the significance of developing a growth mindset and discover key strategies to help you cultivate this mindset and flourish.

First and foremost, understand what a growth mindset entails. A growth mindset is the thought that your abilities, intelligence, and talents can be developed through dedication, effort, and continuous learning. It is the understanding that challenges, setbacks, and failures are opportunities for growth and learning, rather than indicators of limitations. With a growth mindset, you view obstacles as stepping stones and believe in the power of perseverance and effort to overcome them.

To develop a growth mindset, start by reframing your beliefs about your skills and potential. Question the notion that your qualities are outdated and rigid. Embrace the thought that you can improve, learn new skills, and overcome challenges through effort and dedication. Recognise that your intelligence, talents, and skills are not outdated, but rather qualities that can be developed and expanded over time.

Cultivating a growth mindset requires self-awareness and an inclination towards personal growth. Take time to reflect on your current beliefs and attitudes toward challenges, failures, and successes. Identify any outdated mindset, thoughts or beliefs that may be holding you back. Replace these thoughts with positive, growth-oriented affirmations and beliefs. For example, instead of thinking, 'I'm not good at this', shift your mindset to 'I haven't mastered this yet, but with practice, I can improve.'

Embrace a love for learning and a thirst for knowledge. See every experience as an opportunity for growth and learning. Embrace challenges as a chance to broaden your horizon and acquire new skills. View failures as valuable feedback that provides insights for improvement. Embrace a mindset of curiosity, seeking out new experiences and seeking feedback from others. Emphasise the process of learning and personal growth rather than focusing solely on results or external validation.

Developing a growth mindset also requires perseverance and resilience. Understand that success is not achieved overnight and that setbacks and obstacles are part of the journey. Adopt a 'never give up' approach and view failures as temporary setbacks rather than permanent defeats. When faced with challenges, tackle them with a problem-solving mindset, seeking creative solutions and strategies to overcome them. Embrace the idea that effort and hard work are essential for growth and improvement.

Surround yourself with a supportive network of individuals with a growth mindset. Seek out mentors, coaches, or peers who inspire and motivate you to reach your full potential. Engage in collaborative learning and surround yourself with individuals who encourage and motivate you to grow. Share your goals and aspirations with others, as this fosters relationship and support.

Finally, practise self-compassion and embrace a positive mindset. Be kind to yourself and accept that setbacks and failures are a natural part of the learning process. Treat yourself with the same compassion and understanding you would to a friend facing similar challenges. Celebrate your progress and achievements, no matter how small, as this reinforces a positive and growth-oriented mindset.

In conclusion, developing a growth mindset is a transformative journey that empowers you to unlock your potential and achieve greater success. By reframing your beliefs, embracing challenges, cultivating a love for learning, and surrounding yourself with a supportive network, you can cultivate a growth mindset. Embrace the power of perseverance, resilience, and self-compassion as you navigate the ups and downs of your personal and professional endeavours. With a growth mindset, you can continuously learn, grow, and achieve your goals, ultimately reaching new heights of success and fulfilment.

8.4 Embracing Continuous Learning: Fuelling Your Growth and Success

Welcome to the heady world of continuous learning, where knowledge becomes the impetus for personal and professional growth. As an individual committed to growth and success, embracing continuous learning is key to staying relevant, adapting to change, and unlocking new opportunities. In this chapter, we will explore the significance of embracing continuous learning and discover key strategies to help you cultivate a lifelong learning mindset.

First and foremost, understand the power of continuous learning. In today's rapidly evolving world, knowledge and skills quickly become outdated. By embracing continuous learning, you equip yourself with the tools and insights needed to thrive in a dynamic environment. It enables you to stay ahead of the curve, seize new opportunities, and adapt to emerging trends and technologies.

To embrace continuous learning, start by fostering a growth mindset. Believe in your abilities to acquire new knowledge and develop new skills throughout your life. Recognise that learning is not limited to formal education but can occur through various channels, such as reading books, taking workshops, participating in online courses, or seeking mentorship. Consider that your growth potential is limitless.

Make learning a priority in your life. Dedicate time and resources to expand your knowledge and skills. Set specific learning goals and create a plan to achieve them. Incorporate learning into your daily routine, whether by allocating time for reading, listening to educational podcasts during your commute, or participating in online learning platforms. Consistency is the key when it comes to continuous learning.

Adopt a multidisciplinary channel for learning. Seek knowledge and insights from a variety of fields and disciplines. This broadens your perspective and allows you to make connections between seemingly unrelated areas. Explore diverse subjects that pique your curiosity, as this fuels your passion for learning and encourages creative thinking.

Seek out mentors and experts in your field of interest. Learn from their experiences and tap into their wisdom. Engage in meaningful conversations, ask questions, and seek feedback. A mentor can provide guidance, support, and valuable insights that accelerate learning and growth.

Cultivate a habit of reflection. Take time to review and collate what you have learned. Reflect on your experiences, identify key takeaways, and apply them to real-life situations.

This process of reflection helps reinforce your learning and enhances your ability to use knowledge effectively.

Adopt a collaborative approach to learning. Engage in discussions with like-minded individuals, join professional networks or communities, and participate in group learning activities. Collaborative learning allows you to exchange ideas, gain diverse perspectives, and learn from the experiences of others. It fosters a supportive environment that encourages growth and creates opportunities for networking and collaboration.

Embrace technology as a powerful tool for learning. Leverage online resources, e-learning platforms, and digital tools to access a wealth of knowledge. Engage in webinars, podcasts, and online courses to expand your skills and stay abreast with the latest trends in your industry. Embrace digital communities and social media platforms that foster knowledge sharing and facilitate connections with experts and thought leaders.

Finally, practise self-motivation and discipline. Embracing continuous learning requires commitment and dedication. Stay motivated by setting meaningful goals, celebrating your progress, and supporting lifelong learning. Stay disciplined by creating a structured learning routine and holding yourself up to it.

In conclusion, embracing continuous learning is the foundation for personal and professional growth. By cultivating a growth mindset, making learning a priority, seeking diverse knowledge, engaging with mentors and communities, leveraging technology, and practising self-motivation, you can fuel your growth and success. Embark on the journey of lifelong learning, and you will continually expand your horizons, seize new opportunities, and become a lifelong learner who thrives in an ever-changing world.

Building a Strong Visitor Culture
Shaping Your Organisation's Identity

Welcome to the world of organisational leadership, where the strength of your visitor culture sets the tone for success. As a leader, you have the power to shape and nurture a strong visitor culture that fosters employee engagement, fuels innovation, and boosts organisational performance. In this chapter, we will explore the significance of building a strong visitor culture and uncover key strategies to help you cultivate a thriving and cohesive work environment.

9.1 Defining Your Visitor Values: Guiding Principles for Organisational Success

Welcome to the world of business leadership, where the values you instil in your visitor serve as the guiding principles for success. As a leader, it is essential to define and communicate your visitor values, as they shape the culture, behaviour, and decision-making within your organisation. In this chapter, we will explore the significance of defining your visitor values and uncover key strategies to help you establish a strong foundation for organisational success.

First and foremost, understanding the importance of visitor values is critical. Visitor values are the fundamental beliefs and principles that guide the conduct and behaviours of individuals within your organisation. They serve as a compass, influencing the way employees interact with one another, make decisions, and contribute to the overall mission and vision of the company. By defining your visitor values, you create a shared understanding of what is important and establish a strong sense of purpose and identity.

When defining your visitor values, it is essential to involve key stakeholders, such as employees, leaders, and even customers. This collaboration ensures that the values are representative of the organisation as a whole and resonate with the people who contribute to its success. Conduct surveys, focus groups, or workshops to gather input and insights from various perspectives. This inclusive process fosters a sense of ownership and commitment to the values among employees.

To create meaningful and impactful visitor values, consider the following strategies:

- Reflect on your organisation's mission and vision: Your visitor values should align with and support your overall mission and vision. Reflect on the purpose and goals of your organisation and identify the principles that lead towards your desired outcomes. These values should be the foundation upon which your visitor operates.
- Identify the desired behaviours: Consider the behaviours and attitudes you want to promote within your organisation. These behaviours should align with your desired visitor culture and contribute to the achievement of your strategic objectives. For example, if innovation is a priority, one of your values could be 'Embrace creativity and develop a growth mindset.'

- Keep it simple and memorable: Effective visitor values are brief and easy to remember. Avoid long lists of values that may get overwhelming or forgettable. Aim for a limited number of values (typically three to five) that are clear, concise, and meaningful. Make sure they are clearly understood and incorporated into everyday decision-making and actions.
- Lead by example: As a leader, it is essential to embody and model the visitor values in your own conduct and behaviour. Your policies set the tone for the organisation and influence how others perceive and interpret the values. Demonstrate the values through your decisions, interactions, and communication, serving as a role model for employees.
- Integrate values into organisational processes: Embed the visitor values into various aspects of your organisation, including recruitment, performance management, training, and recognition programs. Incorporate the values into job descriptions, interview questions, and performance evaluations to ensure structuring between individual behaviours and the desired values.
- Communicate and reinforce the values: Clearly communicate the visitor values to all employees and stakeholders. Use multiple network channels, such as company-wide meetings, internal newsletters, and digital platforms, to ensure resulting and regular messaging. Celebrate and recognise employees who demonstrate the values, reinforcing their importance and creating a positive feedback loop.
- Continuously evaluate and evolve: Visitor values should not be static. Regularly check their relevance and effectiveness in driving the desired culture and outcomes. Seek feedback from employees and stakeholders to identify areas for regrowth or improvement. Adapt and evolve the values to align with the organisation's changing needs and aspirations.

In conclusion, defining your visitor values is a crucial step in establishing a strong organisational culture and guiding the policies and decision-making within your company. By involving key stakeholders, reflecting on your mission and vision, identifying desired behaviours, keeping the values simple and memorable, leading by example, integrating values into organisational processes, communicating and reinforcing the values, and continuously evaluating and evolving them, you can create a powerful set of guiding principles that shape your company's identity and contribute to its long-term success. By living and applying these values, you inspire and empower your employees, foster a positive work environment, and build a strong foundation for organisational growth and achievement. Remember, your visitor values are not just words on a page; they are the heart and soul of your organisation, driving its culture and shaping its future.

9.2 Fostering a Positive Work Environment: Cultivating a Thriving and Engaged Team

Welcome to the realm of leadership, where creating a positive work environment is crucial for the success and well-being of your team. As a leader, it is your responsibility to foster a workplace culture that promotes collaboration, growth, and happiness. A positive work environment not only enhances employee satisfaction and productivity but also attracts and retains top talent. In this chapter, we will explore the significance of fostering a positive work environment and unveil key strategies to help you cultivate a flourishing and productive team.

A positive work environment is a result of deliberate effort. It requires a proactive commitment to build a culture that prioritises the well-being and satisfaction of your team members. By fostering a positive work environment, you create an atmosphere that empowers individuals to perform at their best and encourages them to develop their skills and reach their full potential.

To cultivate a positive work environment, consider the following strategies:
- Open and Transparent Communication: Establish well-spoken lines of network and encourage open dialogue within your team. Foster an environment where feedback is welcomed and valued. Regularly share information about visitor updates, goals, and challenges. Actively listen to your team members' concerns and suggestions and provide constructive feedback to foster growth and development.
- Respect and Empathy: Treat every team member with respect and empathy. Value their unique perspectives, experiences, and contributions. Encourage a culture of inclusivity and diversity where everyone feels safe, respected, and valued. Foster strong relationships based on trust, support, and understanding.
- Recognition and Appreciation: Acknowledge and appreciate your team members' efforts and achievements. Celebrate milestones and successes, both big and small. Recognise individuals for their contributions and publicly express gratitude. This fosters a sense of belonging and motivation, boosting morale and engagement.
- Work-Life Balance: Encourage a healthy work-life balance among your team members. Support flexible work schedules when possible, letting individuals manage their personal and professional commitments effectively. Promote wellness initiatives and provide resources that support physical and mental well-being.
- Professional Development: Invest in the growth and learning of your team members. Provide opportunities for learning, skill-

building, and career advancement. Offer training programs, mentorship, and coaching to help individuals enhance their skills and reach their professional goals. Encourage a culture of continuous learning and provide resources for personal and career development.

- Collaboration and Teamwork: Foster a collaborative work environment where teamwork is valued and encouraged. Create opportunities for cross-functional collaboration and knowledge sharing. Promote a sense of belonging and unity by organising team-building activities and fostering a supportive and cooperative atmosphere.
- Flexibility and Adaptability: Embrace flexibility and resilience in your work environment. Encourage innovation and creativity by permitting individuals to explore new ideas and approaches. Be open to change and encourage experimentation. Create a culture that values learning from failures and embraces continuous improvement.
- Lead by Example: As a leader, your actions speak louder than words. Model the behaviours and attitudes you want to see in your team members. Demonstrate integrity, professionalism, and a positive attitude. Show empathy, resilience, and adaptability. Lead by example and inspire your team through your own actions and behaviour.

Remember, creating a positive work environment is an ongoing process that requires continuous effort and dedication. Regularly assess the pulse of your team by seeking feedback and conducting employee surveys. Listen to your team members' needs, concerns, and suggestions and make a note of them. Be open to evolving your practices and strategies based on feedback and changing dynamics within your organisation.

In conclusion, fostering a positive work environment is essential for cultivating a thriving and engaged team. By implementing strategies such as open communication, respect and empathy, recognition and appreciation, work-life balance, professional development, collaboration and teamwork, flexibility and adaptability, and leading by example, you can create a work environment that promotes happiness, productivity, and success. Remember, a positive work environment starts with you as a leader. Your commitment, actions, and dedication to cultivating a thriving workplace culture will impact your team members. By fostering a positive work environment, you not only create a place where individuals can thrive and grow, but you also build a strong and engaged team ready to tackle challenges, achieve goals, and contribute to the overall success of your organisation.

9.3 Attracting and Retaining Talent: Strategies for Building a High-Performing Team

Welcome to the world of talent management, where the ability to attract and retain top talent is crucial for the success and growth of your organisation. As a leader, it is essential to create an environment that not only attracts highly skilled individuals but also keeps them engaged, motivated, and dedicated to your organisation's goals. In this chapter, we will explore the significance of attracting and retaining talent and unveil key strategies to help you build a high-performing team.

Attracting and retaining top talent is a competitive endeavour. In today's job market, candidates have numerous options, and organisations must differentiate themselves to stand out. To attract talent, consider the following strategies:

- Employer Branding: Develop a convincing employer brand that reflects your organisation's values, culture, and mission.

Communicate your unique selling points and showcase the opportunities for growth, learning, and impact that your organisation offers. Use various channels, such as social media, career websites, and employee testimonials, to build awareness and attract top talent.

- Competitive Rewards and Benefits: Offer a competitive salary and benefits package that aligns with industry standards. Conduct market research to ensure your reward is attractive to potential candidates. Additionally, consider offering unique perks, such as flexible work schedules, professional learning opportunities, wellness programs, and work-life balance initiatives, to enhance the overall employee experience.
- Strong Visitor Culture: Foster a positive and inclusive visitor culture that values collaboration, innovation, and continuous learning. Create an environment where employees feel empowered, valued, and supported. Encourage open communication, provide growth opportunities, and celebrate achievements. A strong visitor culture not only attracts talent but also contributes to higher employee engagement and retention.
- Robust Recruitment Process: Implement a robust recruitment process that attracts qualified candidates efficiently. Develop articulate job descriptions and selection criteria that clearly reflect the required skills and qualifications. Use multiple recruitment channels, such as job boards, networking events, and employee referrals, to broaden your talent pool. Conduct thorough interviews and assessments to ensure a good fit between candidates and your organisation's values and goals.

Once you have attracted top talent, it is equally important to focus on retaining them. Consider the following strategies to enhance employee retention:

- Opportunities for Growth and Development: Provide articulate pathways for career growth and learning within your organisation. Offer opportunities for training, mentoring, and skill-building that allow employees to expand their knowledge and excel in their careers. Implement performance management systems that provide regular feedback and identify learning opportunities.
- Employee Engagement: Foster a culture of employee engagement by involving employees in decision-making, providing regular opinions and feedback, and recognising their contributions. Create a sense of purpose and structure with the organisation's goals. Encourage autonomy, ownership, and innovation in their roles.
- Work-Life Balance: Promote a healthy work-life balance by offering flexible work schedules, such as remote work options, flexible hours, or compact workweeks. Respect employees' personal time and encourage them to take breaks and vacations to recharge. Support work-life balance initiatives that contribute to their overall well-being.
- Competitive Total Rewards: Regularly evaluate and improve your total rewards package, including compensation, benefits, and recognition programs. Regularly measure your offerings against industry standards to ensure they remain competitive. Provide opportunities for performance-based incentives and recognition to motivate and reward high-performing employees.
- Supportive Leadership and Management: Invest in leadership learning and ensure managers have the skills to support and develop their team members. Foster a supportive and inclusive management style that encourages open communication, trust, and collaboration. Provide opportunities for managers to receive feedback, coaching, and mentorship to enhance their leadership capabilities.

- Employee Well-being: Prioritise employee well-being by providing resources and initiatives that support physical, mental, and emotional health. Offer wellness programs, employee assistance programs, and access to resources for stress management and work-life balance. Create a supportive environment where employees feel cared for.
- Recognition and Rewards: Implement a robust recognition and rewards program to acknowledge and appreciate employee contributions. Recognise achievements and milestones, both individual and team-based, through formal and informal recognition methods. Celebrate success and create a positive and motivating work environment.
- Opportunities for Autonomy and Impact: Provide employees with opportunities to have autonomy in their work and make a meaningful impact. Encourage innovation and creativity by giving individuals the freedom to explore new ideas and take ownership of their projects. Create a culture that values initiative and allows employees to contribute their unique skills and perspectives.
- Strong Leadership Communication: Establish articulate and effective network channels with your team. Regularly share updates, goals, and expectations to keep employees informed and engaged. Be transparent in your communication and encourage open dialogue. Listen actively to your employees' feedback and note their concerns promptly.
- Continuous Feedback and Development: Encourage continuous feedback and learning to promote growth and improvement. Provide regular feedback to your employees, recognising their strengths and areas for improvement. Offer opportunities for skill enhancement and support their professional goals. Encourage a learning mindset and provide resources for continuous learning and development.

In conclusion, attracting and retaining top talent is critical for building a high-performing team. By focusing on strategies such as employer branding, competitive compensation, strong visitor culture, employee engagement, work-life balance, leadership support, employee well-being, recognition and rewards, autonomy and impact, and continuous feedback and development, you can create an environment that attracts top talent and keeps them motivated, engaged, and dedicated to your organisation's success. Remember, talent is a valuable asset, and investing in their satisfaction and growth will yield long-term benefits for your organisation.

9.4 Encouraging Innovation and Collaboration: Unlocking the Power of Creativity and Teamwork

Welcome to the world of innovation and collaboration, where creativity and teamwork are the driving forces behind transformative ideas and ground-breaking solutions. As a leader, it is essential to foster an environment that encourages innovation and collaboration, as they are key ingredients for organisational success and growth. In this chapter, we will explore the significance of encouraging innovation and collaboration and unveil key strategies to help you unlock the power of creativity and teamwork within your team.

Innovation and collaboration are not just buzzwords; they are essential elements for staying competitive and thriving in today's rapidly evolving business landscape. By encouraging innovation, you enable your team to think outside the box, question the status quo, and come up with fresh ideas that can lead to new opportunities and solutions. Collaboration, on the other hand, allows individuals to pool their diverse skills, knowledge, and perspectives, fostering harmony and shared knowledge.

To encourage innovation and collaboration within your team, consider the following strategies:

- Foster a Culture of Psychological Safety: Create an environment where team members feel safe to take risks, share their ideas, and express their opinions without fear of judgement or negative repercussions. Encourage open and honest communication, active listening, and respect for different viewpoints. Acknowledge and learn from failures, emphasising that they are stepping stones to success.
- Establish Well-spoken Goals and Expectations: Clearly communicate the goals and expectations of innovation and collaboration within your team. Set articulate objectives that inspire creativity and foster a sense of purpose. Align these goals with the overall vision and strategy of your organisation. Encourage team members to take ownership of their work and empower them to contribute their unique skills and perspectives.
- Provide Resources and Support: Ensure your team members have the necessary resources, tools, and support to innovate and interact effectively. Provide access to technology, training, and professional learning opportunities that enhance their skills and knowledge. Create a supportive environment where team members can seek guidance, mentorship, and feedback.
- Encourage Cross-functional Collaboration: Promote cross-functional collaboration within your organisation. Encourage team members from different departments or disciplines to work together on projects and initiatives. Foster a culture of knowledge sharing and collaboration by organising brainstorming sessions, workshops, and collaborative problem-solving activities.
- Promote Diversity and Inclusion: Embrace diversity and inclusion within your team. Recognise and acknowledge the unique perspectives, experiences, and backgrounds that each

team member brings to the table. Encourage the exchange of ideas and foster an inclusive environment where everyone's voice is heard and valued. Research shows that diverse teams are increasingly innovative and produce the best outcomes.
- Indulge Time for Creative Thinking: Allot time and space for team members to engage in creative thinking and innovation. Provide opportunities for brainstorming, discussion, and exploration of new ideas. Encourage individuals to step beyond their daily tasks and engage in creative activities such as taking conferences, participating in workshops, or engaging in hobbies.
- Recognise and Reward Innovation and Collaboration: Discuss and celebrate innovative ideas and successful collaborative efforts within your team. Implement a recognition and reward system that reinforces the importance of innovation and collaboration. This can be done through formal recognition programs, incentive structures, or even informal acknowledgements during team meetings. Celebrate individual and team achievements, fostering a culture of appreciation and motivation.
- Lead by Example: As a leader, you play a crucial role in fostering innovation and collaboration. Lead by example and demonstrate the behaviours and attitudes you want to see in your team. Encourage experimentation, embrace new ideas, and show openness to feedback. Foster a culture of learning and continuous improvement by staying receptive to new approaches and encouraging the exploration of different solutions.

In conclusion, encouraging innovation and collaboration is essential for unlocking the full potential of your team and driving organisational success. By fostering a culture that embraces creativity, teamwork, and open communication, you create an environment where innovative ideas can flourish and collaboration can thrive. Implement these strategies and watch your team transform into a powerhouse of innovation, producing remarkable results and propelling your organisation to new heights. Remember, innovation and collaboration are not just individual efforts but a shared journey that requires ongoing support, encouragement, and nurturing. Together, let's unlock the power of creativity and teamwork and build a brighter future for your team and organisation.

Scaling and Exiting Strategies
Navigating Growth and Maximising Opportunities

Welcome to the world of scaling and exiting strategies, where the decisions you make as a leader can shape the future path of your organisation. Scaling involves expanding your business operations to reach new markets, serve more customers, and achieve sustainable growth. Exiting, on the other hand, involves thoughtfully planning and executing a strategic exit from your business, whether through a merger, acquisition, or other means. In this chapter, we will explore the significance of scaling and exiting strategies and unveil key considerations to help you navigate growth and maximise opportunities for your organisation.

10.1 Strategies for Scaling Your Startup: Unlocking Growth and Maximising Potential

Welcome to the world of entrepreneurship, where your startup has taken flight and now faces the exciting question of scaling. Scaling a startup involves navigating the path to growth, expanding your operations, and maximising your organisation's potential. As a startup founder, you need a clear vision and constructive strategies to propel your business forward. In this chapter, we will explore the significance of scaling and unveil key strategies to help you unlock growth and maximise the potential of your startup.

Scaling your startup is a complex and dynamic process that requires careful planning, execution, and adaptation. It involves expanding your consumer base, increasing revenue flow, and optimising your operations to handle growth. By implementing constructive strategies, you can position your startup for success and achieve sustainable growth.

To scale your startup, consider the following strategies:

- Define Your Scaling Strategy: Start by clearly defining your scaling strategy and aligning it with your overall business goals. Determine the areas of your business that you want to scale, such as sales, marketing, operations, or product development. Identify your target market and consumer segments. Develop a roadmap with key milestones and metrics to measure progress.

- Build a Strong Team: Surround yourself with a talented and secure team that shares your vision and values. Invest in hiring and retaining top talent with the skills and expertise required for scaling your startup. Empower your team members, delegate responsibilities, and foster a culture of collaboration and innovation. Encourage continuous learning and provide opportunities for professional development.

- Focus on Consumer Satisfaction and Retention: Develop a comprehensive consumer satisfaction strategy that targets your loyal customers and powerfully communicates the value proposition of your product or service. Leverage various marketing channels, such as digital marketing, content marketing, and social media, to reach your target audience. Implement consumer retention strategies, such as personalised consumer experiences, loyalty programs, and consumer service, to maximise consumer lifetime value.

- Optimise Your Operations: Streamline and optimise your operations to handle increased demand and efficiently deliver your product or service. Identify bottlenecks and inefficiencies in your processes and implement solutions to modernise productivity and scalability. Use technology and automation tools to streamline repetitive tasks and enhance operational efficiency. Continuously monitor and check your operations to identify areas for improvement.
- Foster Strategic Partnerships: Interact with strategic partners who can complement your offerings, expand your reach, or provide access to new markets or distribution channels. Seek partnerships that align with your business objectives and enhance your value proposition. Joint ventures, strategic alliances, or distribution partnerships can accelerate your growth and provide access to new resources and opportunities.
- Secure Sufficient Funding: Scaling your startup requires secure financial resources. Evaluate your funding needs and explore various sources of capital, such as venture capital, kind investors, crowdfunding, or loans. Develop a comprehensive financial plan and forecast to demonstrate the scalability and profitability of your business. Maintain financial strength and regularly review your financial performance to ensure sustainability.
- Embrace Technology and Innovation: Leverage technology to boost efficiency, innovation, and scalability. Stay updated with the latest industry trends, emerging technologies, and groundbreaking innovations that can enhance your product or service. Embrace a culture of innovation within your organisation, encourage idea generation from your team members, and explore new avenues for growth and differentiation.
- Monitor Key Metrics and Learn from Data: Establish KPIs

and metrics that align with your scaling objectives. Regularly monitor and check these metrics to track progress, identify trends, and make data-driven decisions. Use data analytics to gain insights into consumer behaviour, market trends, and operational performance. Use these insights to optimise your strategies and improve when necessary.

In conclusion, scaling your startup is a journey that requires careful planning, strategic decision-making, and the implementation of constructive strategies. By defining your scaling strategy, building a strong team, focusing on consumer satisfaction and retention, optimising your operations, fostering strategic partnerships, securing sufficient funding, embracing technology and innovation, and monitoring key metrics, you can unlock growth and maximise the potential of your startup. Remember, scaling is not a one-size-fits-all process, so be consistent and willing to improvise as you navigate the exciting path to growth and success. With the right strategies and a dedicated team, your startup can thrive and make a lasting impact in the marketplace.

10.2 Investment and Acquisition Opportunities: Making Informed Decisions for Business Growth

Welcome to the world of investment and acquisitions, where the pursuit of strategic opportunities can propel your business to new heights. As a decision-maker, it is crucial to possess the skills and knowledge required to evaluate investment and acquisition opportunities effectively. This process involves careful analysis, due diligence, and a thorough understanding of the potential risks and rewards involved. In this chapter, we will explore the significance of evaluating investment and acquisition opportunities and unveil key strategies to help you make informed decisions for business growth.

Evaluating investment and acquisition opportunities requires discipline and a comprehensive understanding of your organisation's strategic objectives. It is essential to align potential opportunities with your long-term vision and goals. By raising a systematic evaluation process, you can minimise risks and maximise the chances of success.

To evaluate investment and acquisition opportunities, consider the following strategies:

- Clearly Define Your Investment Criteria: Define the criteria that align with your investment strategy. Determine the specific industries, markets, or companies relevant to your organisation. Establish financial criteria, such as minimum return on investment (ROI) or specific valuation metrics, to guide your decision-making process. Clear investment criteria will help you filter and focus on opportunities that align with your strategic objectives.
- Self-mastery Thorough Due Diligence: Be diligent to gain a comprehensive understanding of the investment or acquisition target. Evaluate the target company's financial performance, market position, competitive landscape, growth potential, and any legal or regulatory considerations. Assess the target's assets, liabilities, and intellectual property. Engage professionals, such as financial advisors, legal experts, and industry consultants, to assist with the process.
- Assess Cultural and Strategic Fit: Evaluate the cultural and strategic fit between your organisation and the potential investment or acquisition target. Assess whether the target's values, mission, and organisational culture align with yours. Consider how the acquisition or investment will complement your existing operations and improve your competitive advantage. A strong cultural and strategic fit is crucial for successful integration and long-term value creation.

- Evaluate Potential Teamwork: Identify potential collaboration or teamwork through investment or acquisition. Assess how the target company's resources, capabilities, and market access can complement your own. Evaluate the potential for forfeit savings, revenue growth, and market expansion. Consider how operations, technologies, or distribution networks can create value and accelerate business growth.
- Check Financial Viability: Carefully check the financial viability of the investment or acquisition opportunity. Assess the target company's historical and projected financial performance, cash flow, profitability, and debt levels. Evaluate the quality of its assets, including any intangible resources such as patents or brand value. Consider the potential impact on your organisation's financial position, wanted structure, and return on investment.
- Evaluate Risks and Acquisition Strategies: Identify and assess the potential risks associated with the investment or acquisition opportunity. Consider market risks, regulatory risks, operational risks, and integration risks. Develop mitigation strategies to note and minimise these risks. Assess the potential impact on your organisation's reputation and trademark value. Consider the scenarios and stress testing to evaluate the resilience of your investment or acquisition in different market conditions.
- Seek Expert Opinion and Perspective: Engage external experts, like financial advisors, legal counsels, or industry specialists, to provide objective opinions and perspectives. These professionals can bring valuable insights and expertise to the evaluation process. They can assist with financial analysis, legal aspects, and market research. Their expertise can help you make well-informed decisions and mitigate potential risks.
- Consider Long-Term Value Creation: Evaluate the potential for long-term value creation through investment or acquisition.

Consider how the opportunity aligns with your organisation's growth strategy and the potential for expanding market presence, diversifying product offerings, or entering new markets. Assess the competitive advantages and unique capabilities that the investment or acquisition can bring to your organisation. Consider the scalability and sustainability of the opportunity, as well as the potential for generating long-term returns on investment.

In conclusion, evaluating investment and acquisition opportunities is critical for business growth. By clearly defining your investment criteria, conducting thorough research, assessing cultural and strategic fit, evaluating potential collaboration and teamwork, analysing financial viability, assessing risks, seeking expert advice, and considering long-term value creation, you can make informed decisions that align with your organisation's goals and maximise the potential for success. Remember that each opportunity is unique, and a systematic evaluation process will help you navigate the complexities and uncertainties of the investment and acquisition landscape. With careful analysis and strategic decision-making, you can unlock growth opportunities and boost your business towards success.

10.3 Planning for a Successful Exit: Navigating the Path to a Rewarding Transition

Welcome to the world of business, where every journey has a destination, and planning for a successful exit is an essential part of the entrepreneurial experience. As a business owner, it is crucial to have a clear vision and constructive strategies to ensure a smooth transition when the time comes to exit your venture. Whether you're considering a sale, merger, or passing on the reins to a successor, proper planning is the key to maximising the value of your business and achieving a rewarding exit. In this chapter, we will explore the significance of planning for a successful exit and unveil key strategies to help you navigate the path to a fulfilling transition.

Planning for a successful exit is not a one-size-fits-all process. It requires careful consideration of your personal and business goals and the exact circumstances surrounding your exit. A strategic and proactive approach can help position your business for a successful transition and ensure a rewarding outcome.

To plan for a successful exit, consider the following strategies:

- Define Your Exit Strategy: Start by clearly defining your exit strategy and aligning it with your long-term goals. Determine the potential outcome for your business, whether it's a sale to a strategic buyer, a merger with a complementary company, an initial public offering (IPO), or a succession plan. Consider the timeline for your exit and the financial goals you wish to achieve. A definite exit strategy will guide your decision-making and help you focus on your desired outcome.
- Prepare Your Business for Sale: If you're considering a sale as your exit strategy, it's essential to prepare your business for the transaction. Conduct a thorough research of your company's financials, operations, and market position. Identify areas for improvement and implement strategies to increase the value of your business. Streamline your operations, strengthen your financial performance, and ensure that your intellectual property and legal matters are in order. Presenting a well-prepared and attractive business to potential buyers can increase your chances of securing a favourable sale.
- Build a Strong Management Team: A strong management team is crucial for a successful exit. Invest in building a capable and

experienced team that can run the business effectively, even without your direct involvement. Delegate responsibilities, provide training and mentorship, and foster a culture of dedication and performance. Demonstrating a capable management team to potential buyers or successors adds value to your business and instils conviction in its prospects.

- Seek Professional Advice: Engage experienced professionals, such as business brokers, investment bankers, or legal and financial advisors, to guide you through the exit planning process. These experts can provide valuable insights, help navigate complex legal and financial considerations, and assist with negotiations. Their expertise can help you optimise the terms of your exit and ensure a smooth transition.
- Identify and Nurture Potential Buyers or Successors: If you're looking to sell your business or pass it on to a successor, it's essential to identify and cultivate potential buyers or successors early on. Build relationships with strategic buyers, investors, or individuals within your industry who may be interested in acquiring your business. If you're considering internal succession, identify and groom potential successors within your organisation. Provide mentoring and learning opportunities to prepare them for future leadership roles.
- Create a Succession Plan: If your exit involves passing on the reins to a successor, it's crucial to develop a comprehensive succession plan. Clearly define the roles and responsibilities of the successor, establish a timeline for the transition, and ensure a smooth transfer of knowledge and relationships. Communicate your vision and expectations, and involve the successor in the key decision-making processes. A well-executed succession plan minimises disruptions and ensures continuity for your business.
- Preserve and Leverage Intellectual Property: Intellectual property, such as patents, trademarks, copyrights, and trade

secrets, can significantly increase the value of your business. Protect and leverage your intellectual property resources throughout the exit planning process. Inspect your intellectual property portfolio, ensure proper documentation and legal protection, and explore opportunities to license or monetise your intellectual property. Demonstrating a robust intellectual property strategy can attract potential buyers and increase the overall value of your business.

- Communicate Effectively: Effective communication is vital during the exit planning process. Keep stakeholders, including employees, customers, suppliers, and investors, informed about your intentions and the progress of your exit plans. Transparent and open communication helps build trust and maintain the goodwill of your business. Develop a communication plan that outlines key messages, timing, and the appropriate channels for sharing information. By proactively managing communication, you can mitigate uncertainties and maintain positive relationships with key stakeholders.
- Manage Personal Finances: As you plan for a successful exit, it's essential to consider your personal financial goals and ensure financial security beyond your business. Evaluate your personal financial situation, including savings, investments, and retirement plans. Engage with financial advisors to create a comprehensive personal financial plan that aligns with your desired lifestyle and future aspirations. By managing your personal finances effectively, you can confidently navigate the transition and focus on the next instalment of your life.
- Plan for Life, Without the Exit: Finally, don't forget to plan for life without the exit. Exiting your business can be emotionally and mentally challenging, especially if you have dedicated a significant part of your life to its success. Take time to reflect on your personal goals, hobbies, and interests outside the business

realm. Consider engaging in new ventures, philanthropic activities, or mentorship opportunities. Planning for a fulfilling and purposeful life without the exit can help you transition smoothly and embrace the next phase of your journey.

In conclusion, planning for a successful exit is a crucial step in the entrepreneurial journey. By defining your exit strategy, preparing your business, building a strong management team, seeking professional advice, identifying potential buyers or successors, creating a succession plan, leveraging intellectual property, communicating effectively, managing personal finances, and planning for life without the exit, you can navigate the path to a rewarding transition. Remember, a well-planned exit not only maximises the value of your business but also sets the stage for new opportunities and personal fulfilment.

10.4 Transitioning to the Next Chapter: Embracing Change and Discovering New Possibilities

Welcome to the threshold of change, where one instalment ends and a new one begins. Transitioning to the next instalment of your life is an exciting and transformative journey filled with opportunities for growth, self-discovery, and personal fulfilment. Whether you are embarking on a new career path, starting a family, pursuing remoter education, or simply seeking a fresh start, navigating this transition requires reflection, adaptation, and a willingness to embrace change. In this chapter, we will explore the significance of transitioning to the next instalment and unveil key strategies to help you navigate this transformative process.

Transitioning to the next instalment is a strictly personal and unique experience. It is an opportunity to redefine yourself, explore new passions, and shape the direction of your life. By accepting this transition with intention and openness, you can create a fulfilling and purpose-driven life.

To successfully transition to the next chapter, consider the following strategies:

- Reflect on Your Values and Priorities: Reflect on your values, aspirations, and priorities. Ask yourself what truly matters to you and what you want to prioritise in the next phase of your life. Consider your personal and professional goals, relationships, health, and overall well-being. Aligning your choices and conduct with your personal values and priorities will guide you towards a more meaningful and fulfilling next chapter.
- Embrace Self-Discovery: Transition periods provide an opportunity for self-discovery and personal growth. Utilise this time to explore your passions, interests, and talents. Engage in activities that ignite your curiosity and bring you joy. Experiment with new hobbies, take on new challenges and step outside your comfort zone. Self-discovery allows you to unravel new facets of yourself and discover subconscious talents or interests that can shape your next chapter.
- Set Clear Goals and Create a Plan: Once you have clarity on your values and priorities, set clear goals for your next chapter. Define what success means to you and outline the steps needed to achieve your goals. Create a plan that includes milestones, timelines, and multiple steps. Breaking your goals into manageable tasks will make the transition more practical and achievable.
- Embrace Change and Adaptability: Transition periods are characterised by change, and accepting change is essential for growth. Cultivate a mindset of flexibility and resilience. Be open to new possibilities, even if they differ from your initial expectations. Embrace uncertainty as an opportunity for personal and professional development. Flexibility and

resilience will enable you to navigate unforeseen challenges and seize new opportunities that crop up during the transition.
- Seek Support and Build a Network: Surround yourself with a supportive network of friends, family, mentors, and like-minded individuals who can provide guidance, encouragement, and feedback during your transition. Find mentors or individuals who have successfully navigated similar transitions and learn from their experiences. Connect with professional networks, attend workshops, or join communities that align with your new chapter. A strong support system will provide the emotional and practical support needed to navigate this transformative journey.
- Invest in Self-Care and Well-being: Prioritise self-care and well-being as you transition to the next chapter. Take charge of your physical, mental, and emotional health. Maintain a healthy lifestyle by incorporating exercise, healthy eating, mindfulness, and relaxation techniques into your routine. Take time for self-reflection, self-care activities, and nurturing your relationships. By prioritising self-care, you will have the energy and resilience needed to thrive in your new chapter.
- Stay Curious and Continuously Learn: Never stop learning and stay curious. Find opportunities for personal and professional growth. Pursue distance education, attend workshops, or engage in online courses that align with your interests and goals. Stay updated with industry trends and developments to remain relevant in your chosen path. Embrace a growth mindset and view every experience as an opportunity for learning and development. Continuously expanding your knowledge and skills will not only enrich your personal journey but also improve your prospects.
- Embrace Flexibility and Adaptation: Transitioning to the next instalment often involves navigating uncertainties and unexpected changes. Embrace the inherent flexibility of this process and be open to adjusting your plans on the way. Stay attuned to your

own needs, and be willing to modify your goals or explore new directions as you gain new insights and experiences. Flexibility and resilience are vital qualities that will enable you to navigate the twists and turns of your journey smoothly.
- Practice Gratitude and Positivity: Transition periods can be challenging, but practising gratitude and cultivating a positive mindset can significantly impact your experience. Take time to fathom the progress you have made and the lessons you have learned throughout your journey. Celebrate even the smallest of victories and open the positive aspects of your new chapter. Cultivating a grateful and positive mindset will empower you to embrace the transition with optimism and resilience.
- Embrace the Journey: Remember that transitioning to the next instalment is not only about reaching a destination; it is also about embracing the journey itself. Embrace the ups and downs, the challenges and triumphs, and the growth and self-discovery that come with this transformative process. Cherish the moments of uncertainty and the opportunities for personal evolution. Each step of the journey is a valuable part of your overall growth and contributes to shaping the person you are becoming.

In conclusion, transitioning to the next instalment is a profound and transformative experience that opens doors to new possibilities and personal fulfilment. By reflecting on your values, embracing self-discovery, setting clear goals, and seeking support, you can navigate this transition with intention and purpose. Embrace change, prioritise self-care, and stay open to continuous learning and adaptation. Remember to practice gratitude and maintain a positive mindset throughout your journey. Embrace the unknown, trust in your abilities, and embark on this next instalment with excitement and a sense of adventure. The possibilities are endless, and the path ahead is yours to create.

Appendix
Resources and Tools

A. Recommended Books and Blogs:
- Ries, Eric, *The Lean Startup*.
- Thiel, Peter, *Zero to One*.
- Kahneman, Daniel, *Thinking, Fast and Slow*.
- Blank, Steve, *The Four Steps to the Epiphany*.
- Harvard Business Review, *HBR's 10 Must Reads on Strategy*.
- Sinek, Simon, *Start With Why*.
- Blank, Steve, Dorf, Bob, *The Startup Owner's Manual*.
- Christensen, Clayton M., *The Innovator's Dilemma*.

B. Entrepreneurial Organisations and Networks:
- Entrepreneur's Organisation (EO)
- Young Entrepreneur Council (YEC)
- Startup Grind
- Women's Business Enterprise National Council (WBENC)
- National Association of Women Business Owners (NAWBO)
- Small Business Association (SBA)
- Chambers of Commerce (Local and Regional)

C. Useful Online Tools and Software:

- Trello: A project management tool for organising and tracking tasks.
- Slack: A networking platform for team collaboration and messaging.
- Canva: A graphic designing tool for creating visual content and marketing materials.
- Google Analytics: A web analytics tool for tracking website traffic and user behaviour.
- Mailchimp: An email marketing platform for designing and sending newsletters and campaigns.
- QuickBooks: Written software for managing finances and bookkeeping.
- Asana: A task management tool for tracking and organising projects.
- Zoom: A video conferencing tool for virtual meetings and webinars.
- Buffer: A social media management platform for scheduling and analysing posts.
- Evernote: A note-taking and organisation tool for capturing ideas and information.

These resources and tools can provide valuable insights, guidance, and practical support to improve your entrepreneurial journey, personal growth, and business success. They offer a wealth of knowledge, connections, and capabilities to help you navigate challenges, stay informed, and optimise your strategies and processes. Remember to adapt and explore resources based on your specific needs and interests.